THE UNIVERSITY OF MICHIGAN
CENTER FOR CHINESE STUDIES

MICHIGAN PAPERS IN CHINESE STUDIES

NINETEENTH CENTURY CHINA:

FIVE IMPERIALIST PERSPECTIVES

Selected by Dilip Basu

Edited and with an introduction by Rhoads Murphey

Ann Arbor

Center for Chinese Studies
The University of Michigan

1972

Michigan Papers in Chinese Studies No. 13

Open access edition funded by the National Endowment for the Humanities/ Andrew W. Mellon Foundation Humanities Open Book Program.

Printed in the United States of America

ISBN 978-0-89264-013-3 (hardcover)
ISBN 978-0-472-03801-5 (paper)
ISBN 978-0-472-12741-2 (ebook)
ISBN 978-0-472-90136-4 (open access)

TABLE OF CONTENTS

INTRODUCTION

by

Rhoads Murphey

Efforts to reconstruct the past, and to understand it, must depend on the survival of materials. What survives is partly haphazard, partly the result of varying circumstances of time and place, and partly of the attitudes of those responsible for creating, maintaining, and preserving records and other documents. But attitudes change, and what may seem of little consequence to some at certain times may become highly significant to others at other times. Even the Chinese were far from either recording or preserving everything, and each dynastic group of officials and scholars made a selection of what was considered important, discarding far more than they kept. What survives from traditional China is not necessarily what contemporary scholars would have chosen to preserve -- or to have recorded or studied in the first place.

Some of the materials from the past which tend often to be overlooked are those which wrongly anticipate the future or which present information or judgements which were later proved to be misleading or erroneous. And yet such documents are as legitimate, and perhaps as important, a sample of the period from which they come as others whose material has been vindicated by events or whose perspectives do not jar with those of later generations. Changing perspectives constitute of course the other dimension of the process by which successive generations re-write history. Some things become newly significant and others less so; equally important, each new group of scholars looks for and selects different things, in addition to interpreting the same things differently. Every piece of historical reconstruction is written for its own present. It cannot and perhaps should not be otherwise, but it is useful to remember that this is so, and at the same time to guard against the extremes of mis-representing the past in its own terms. One common risk of doing so results from the effort to discover in the past the seeds of the present. They are there, of course, but they are far from being the whole of the past.

The five documents reproduced here are each typical of the periods from which they come, but none of them represents what might be called the main stream in the sense that each was overtaken or contradicted by events. Given the legitimacy of attempting to see every period as much as possible in its own terms, if not (since that is impossible) wie es eigentlich gewesen, it is important to consider at least a representative sample of everything which was written or recorded: in this case, what China looked like and suggested to Englishmen on the spot in Canton and

Hong Kong in the first half of the nineteenth century, and how they viewed their own country and its role vis-a-vis the China they observed. The first account, by Samuel Ball, was originally printed as a pamphlet in Macao in 1817, and as a consequent piece of ephemera was fortuitously preserved in the Public Records Office in London. The other four accounts, from 1838, 1845, 1847, and 1848, have never before been printed and also found their way, as holographs, to the P.R.O. None of them enjoyed much currency after they were written, for the kinds of reasons discussed above. They were seen at the P.R.O. by Professor Dilip Basu, now of the University of California at Santa Cruz, while he was doing research in London in 1970. He recognized their interest and importance, in the terms already discussed, made xerox copies of each, and, during his term as a Research Associate of the Center for Chinese Studies at Michigan in 1971, loaned them to me to read in connection with my own research on this period, one in which our interests coincide and overlap. We agreed on the usefulness of making them available to a wider audience.

The servants of the East India Company at their Canton factory included many who, like their compatriots in India, made a serious effort to learn and to understand something of the country and civilization on whose margins they conducted their business. After the early Jesuits, they represent the beginning of modern Western efforts to study China and the Chinese. Some of them learned more or less of the language, and a few, including the authors of the first two pieces reproduced here, went so far as to include some Chinese characters and even references to Chinese sources in what they wrote. A small handful, more daring, disguised themselves as Chinese (after taking their Chinese servants or travelling companions into their confidence) and made information-collecting trips inland before the post-1842 treaty provisions made this officially possible. Whatever their points of view or motives, Westerners were widely curious about China, especially the Westerners on the spot, while the Chinese were much less interested in them or in the countries and cultures from which they came. Part of the imperialist mind consisted in this eagerness to explore the world, to get a picture of all of its parts -- and as rapidly as possible to "open" all areas to the beneficent influence of the West, notably through an expanded commerce as the sovereign medium of cultural interchange which would also enrich its Western masters.

About 60 per cent has been selected from the originals of Samuel Ball's pamphlet and the anonymous account, "A Dissertation Upon the Commerce of China", leaving out extensive sections of factual description of the landscapes, products, and towns of each of China's provinces, most of it apparently based on published works which are still available but adding nothing to existing knowledge. R. M. Martin's shorter essay is reproduced here in its entirety. The fourth document, an exchange of correspondence in 1847 about British access to and use of land in the vicinity of Canton, has been edited to remove some repetition (primarily the summary by Harry Parkes, which adds nothing); the final piece, on the Morrison Education Society, is set forth in full. Obvious errors of spelling, punctuation, and grammar in each of the originals have been corrected, and in a few cases archaic spellings which might confuse a contemporary reader have been altered to conform with contemporary usage.

Samuel Ball's "Observations" show how much detailed information (and some misinformation) was available to the Westerners even under the Canton system, and elaborates what it was which the British, with their mercantile mind, were after. Du Halde, Staunton, Barrow, and other existing published works readily available at the time provided a good deal of factual information as well as commentary. But the calculations of a British merchant, leading Ball in this case to fix on Foochow as the optimal port for maximizing British access to the trade of China, led him very wide of the mark, as subsequent experience was to prove. Admittedly, he was hampered by incomplete and inaccurate information about important areas and ports, notably Shanghai, and perhaps he is also not to be faulted too harshly for failing to anticipate the relative decline in the importance of tea in China's foreign trade. But too narrow a set of computations appears to have led him to overlook some more important matters, most pointedly the enormous relative advantage enjoyed by Shanghai, Canton, and later Hankou and Tientsin in terms of their ease of access as well as nearness to the bulk of the China market and to its major sources of export goods. China is a huge and enormously productive country; the presence of a cluster of prosperous merchants and the existence of a substantial seaborne trade in one of its hundreds of cities (which Ball happened to know about because it was a southeast coastal port) was of far less significance than he apparently realized. In practice, Foochow, opened as one of the first five treaty ports by the Treaty of Nanking in 1842, never became a place of more than third-rank importance in China's foreign trade or of the Western role in that trade. The tea which Ball counted on moved out largely via Shanghai and Canton, by cheap and heavily travelled water routes; ironically, Foochow was relatively less important as a treaty port than it had been in Ball's day. His account does provide a good deal of interesting detail on the tea trade and its carriage, as well as a more general picture of foreign commerce in the second decade of the nineteenth century.

"A Dissertation Upon the Commerce of China" provides an example of Western perceptions of China on the eve of the first Anglo-Chinese war. It is also an early statement of what appears still to be the deathless dream of the China market as El Dorado: an immense population of eager traders, hard workers, and willing buyers. Internal evidence fixes the date unmistakably as 1838, but the authorship is difficult to assign. By that time there were a great many Englishmen in China, many of whom could well have written this account.

R.M. Martin was Treasurer for the Colonial, Consular, and Diplomatic Service in China and a member of the Hong Kong Legislative Council at the time he wrote the present essay. It is a striking and very early statement of Western imperialism and of the imperial mind, which foreshadows the arguments, rationalizations, and attitudes of fifty years later. Martin published a book, China: Political, Commercial and Social in two volumes, London, 1847, but it contains very little which duplicates the present essay except for the ill-judged remarks about the future of Hong Kong, the substance of which he repeated in his published book.

The correspondence about the series of negotiations with the Chinese authorities over the various pieces of property at Honan (downriver from Canton) is of some interest as a sidelight on the far more pressing "Canton City Question" which was already looming, and as an illustration of the nature of the problems which the newly expanded foreign presence, power, and ambition in China produced, confronting Chinese reluctance, temporizing, and stonewalling. The British at this point were still feeling their way, and were apparently willing to accept, at least temporarily, the impasse in which they found themselves in this matter by August of 1947. This collection of correspondence and reports as preserved at the P.R.O. breaks off with Parkes's "Memorandum" and there is thus no hint of the tensions and conflicts which were to follow, except perhaps for some evidence of divided opinions on the British side about the best way to proceed in establishing in practice the rights supposedly conferred by the Treaty of Nanking. There are some parallels here with the similar problems encountered at about the same time at Shanghai, as in the early years of most of the major treaty port settlements. The "Honan Question" at Canton is perhaps better known but the present collection may serve as a valuable footnote.

The short statement and appeal which forms the final piece was issued in 1848 by the Trustees of the Morrison Education Society and provides a vivid sample of another aspect of Western ambitions and dreams. The Society's problems were to become familiar through nearly a century of varied missionary efforts to achieve the same goals -- and to raise the necessary financial support. Chinese resistance to Western efforts at "civilization" was to be overcome by a combination of Christian evangelism and English education; once thus having been shown the light, surely even the proud Chinese would not choose to continue in "backwardness". In some ways this short text is the most in tune of the five with the events and attitudes of the ensuing century. An extensive, and to some degree a successful, missionary enterprise in education did grow from this early seed. By comparison with the dreams of the foreign traders, it did make a significant impact on the Chinese mind, if not exactly of the sort which Westerners, especially the evangelists, intended. But in this respect, as with all of the other foreign ambitions of the era of imperialism in China, China remained unconquered.

SAMUEL BALL

OBSERVATIONS ON THE EXPEDIENCY OF OPENING A NEW PORT IN CHINA

Macao, 1817

The importance of opening a Second Port in China, as connected with the Company's interests, has escaped the attention of few Persons who have given the least consideration to our connections with that country. Unfortunately, however, there exists so much diversity of opinion as to which Port would be the most favorable that we are involved nearly in the same doubt and perplexity as if nothing had been written upon the subject. Some have fixed on Amoy, others on Ning-po, some on Shang-hay-hien in Kiang-nan, some on Chusan, and Formosa, and some even on Cochin-china. It is to be regretted that none of the advocates for those Ports have stated their reasons of preference more at large, nor is it easy to perceive upon what principles they are grounded. If they be tried by the first great rule in Commerce, viz., to choose the Point where we are best enabled to buy the cheapest and sell the dearest, none will appear to have much weight.

Tea may be considered as the only valuable branch of our Trade, and all our Imports are subservient to the Purchase of this Article. Let it be remembered that scarcely a single Article of the Company's Imports, except Cotton, would ever be brought to China but for the purchase of Tea. It therefore appears probable, even without any examination, that the Port to which the Teas can be sent at the least expense must be the best situation for the Company's trade. If the trade were perfectly unrestrained, no inquiry would be necessary; but since it is diverted from its natural course by the arbitrary regulations of the Government, if we seek any amelioration we must endeavour to determine what the natural channels would be, provided the trade were left free.

Many preliminary objects must therefore be discussed before we can arrive at any solid conclusions upon this subject. We must first determine which are the Great Rivers of the Empire; through which Provinces they flow; where they disembogue into the sea; how they are connected with other smaller Rivers; and whether and where they form a junction; what are the most Populous Districts; what cities or towns are principally connected with the consumption of our Imports; and which are the seats of the growth and manufacture of the goods we export. When we have determined the relative importance of these, we shall then be enabled to ascertain which Port will be the most favorable for the Trade.

The present inquiry will therefore be conducted upon these principles, and I think I shall be enabled to prove that Canton is of all other Ports the most unfavorable for the trade, and that a Port hitherto unknown or unnamed, that of Fu-chew-fu in the Province of Fo-kien, in the immediate vicinity of the Tea country, is the most favorable.

As the great River, the Yang-cse-kiang, running through the centre of the Empire connects its Western and Eastern extremities in the Province of Kiang-nan, so also do the Yellow River and the Grand Canal unite this Province with the city of Peking, the capital of the Empire, and the Provinces of the North. The Cien-tang-kiang, which flows past the city of Hang-chew-fu, connects this Province again with the Rivers of Che-kiang, Kiang-sy, Quang-tong, and Fo-kien, thus forming a grand communication with all the great Rivers and Canals of the Empire, and uniting in the Eastern Division of the Province of Kiang-nan the Northern and Southern as well as the Western and Eastern extremities of the Empire, a circumstance which has in all ages rendered this particular district eminently Populous and Commercial. No less than five cities of the first order, among which are the celebrated ones of Su-chew-fu and Hang-chew-fu, are seated on the banks of that part of the Grand Canal which lies between the bason at Hang-chew-fu and its junction with the Yang-cse-kiang, a distance of only 200 miles, besides Nan-king, the ancient capital of the Empire, the cities of Song-kiang-fu and Keu-chew-fu, and innumerable towns and hamlets in its immediate vicinity.

It appears that the cities or towns principally connected with the Foreign Trade are all within the influence of the Yang-cse-kiang and the Grand Canal, except those of Quong-tong, Quong-sy, and Fo-kien, and that even the Tea Districts in this latter Province are considerably nearer that River and the Grand Canal than to Canton; also, that the facilities of communication with any of these cities or towns by means of the Yang-cse-kiang and the Grand Canal are greater, and the navigation better, than from Canton to the same places.

<u>The Relative Importance of the Principal Marts</u>. The Company's Imports into China consist of Cotton, Woollens, Lead, Iron, and Tin; the Exports, of Black and Green Tea, Raw Silk, and Nankeens.

Cotton. The Bombay Cotton is at present entirely manufactured and principally consumed in the two provinces of Quong-tong and Quong-sy. The Bengal Cotton is partly consumed in the same Provinces, but principally sent to Fo-kien, where it is manufactured and consumed.

Woollens. It appears that the greatest quantity of Woollens is sent to the two Principal Marts of Commerce before described, viz., Han-keu in Hu-quoang and Hang-chew-fu in Che-kiang; and that the whole quantity, except such part as is intended for the consumption of Quong-tong, Quong-sy, and Fokien, is sent to the before mentioned Provinces of Hu-quong, Kiang-sy, Kiang-nan, and Che-kiang, all within the influence of the great River the Yang-cse-kiang and the Grand Canal, or to the Provinces North of these. Consequently, the River Yang-cse-kiang, or the city of Han-chew-fu, would be more favorable situations than Canton for the diffusion of the Woollens over the Empire, except such as are intended for the immediate consumption of the two Provinces of Canton and of Quong-sy.

Lead. The lead is chiefly consumed at Canton, this being an article that will not bear the expense of transport. A small quantity is sent annually to the Green Tea Districts, but none to Fo-kien; the people of this Province purchase their lead at Han-keu, and the expense of carriage being about one half of that from Canton is the reason why this lead is preferred.

Tin and Iron. Tin is also principally consumed at Canton; a small quantity, however, is also annually sent to the Green Tea Districts. Iron will not bear the expense of transport, and is therefore consumed at Canton.

Now supposing the Trade with China to be rendered a Free Trade, it would probably settle itself into five Ports or Divisions, viz., one in the Gulph of Pe-chy-ly; a second at the mouth of the River Yang-cse-kiang in Kiang-nan; a third at Hang-chew-fu in Che-kiang; a fourth at Fu-chew-fu in Fo-kien; and a fifth at Canton. The quantity and amount of Company's Imports actually consumed in the present state of the Trade in each of these Divisions, and the quantity and amount of Exports that could be most conveniently shipped from the same places are as follows:

IMPORTS*			EXPORTS	
Districts	Quantity of Woollens	Amount of Sales at Canton		Amount of Purchases at Canton
Pe-chy-ly	one-ninth	270,552		
Yang-cse-kiang	three-fifths	1,488,036		
Hang-chew-fu	one-ninth	270,552	Green Tea, Raw Silk, and Nankeens	1,759,023
Fo-kien†	-----	-----	Black Tea, consisting of two thirds of the Exports	3,762,660
Canton Ditto Cotton Ditto Lead and Iron	one-sixth	1,051,708		
Tales		3,080,848		
Add Long Ells, and other Woollens unaccounted for		171,632		
Tales		3,252,480	Tales	5,521,683

*Imports for Season 1814, 15.

†The woollens annually sent to Fo-kien have been added to Hang-chew-fu.

Thus it appears that the Port of Canton is not naturally connected with any part of the Export Trade, and is useful merely for the consumption of Imports suited to this Province and that of Quong-sy. If so large a proportion of Woollens as one-sixth, and Imports generally, are consumed in these two Provinces, it arises merely from this principle: that whatever Port is rendered the general Emporium of the Trade, there will there exist a greater consumption of Foreign Imports, compared with its Population, than in any other part of the Empire. A Port in the Gulph of Pe-chy-ly could only be favorable for the introduction of articles suited to the consumption of the three Provinces of Pe-chy-ly, Shan-sy, and Shan-tong. The city of Hang-chew-fu is the most favorable situation for the exportation of the Green Teas, Raw silk, and Nankeens, and is also a good situation for the introduction of goods for general consumption. But the two most natural and best Ports in the Empire are the Yang-cse-kiang, which carried off three-fifths of the Woollens, and the Province of Fo-kien, which produces two-thirds of the Exports.

Thus, as far as population, wealth, actual consumption, and easy transport of goods are concerned, a Port in the Eastern Division of the Province of Kiang-nan, at that point where the River Yang-cse-kiang cuts the Grand Canal, is the best geographical situation for the introduction of all goods suited to general consumption, and might perhaps be the most favorable one for the trade, but for the bulk and great expense of transporting the Balck Tea out of the Province of Fo-kien. *

Fo-kien is divided from the adjacent Provinces by a chain of mountains that renders the transport of goods exceedingly expensive. The Passes over which the Teas are carried into the Province of Kiang-sy, and from thence to Canton, lie to the North of Csong-ngan-hien, where the River Min ceases to be navigable. The expense of Porterage across these Mountains amounts to one Tale two Mace five Candareens per Pecul, which is more than one-third of the whole carriage, though this Pass is not one-seventh of the whole distance, nor the time occupied one-fifth of the whole time necessary for the transport of Teas to Canton. Such is the expense of this land journey, which is the usual route for conveying the Teas to the other Provinces. Nor can the Teas be moved out of this Province without incurring an expense of carriage of five times the amount necessary for shipping them from the Port of Fu-chew-fu. But the greater the expense of crossing these Mountains, the more necessary

*It is doubtful whether the Rivers Yang-cse-kiang and Cien-tang-kiang are accessible to Ships of heavy burthen. In that case the port of Shang-hay-hien, recommended by Mr. Pigou, becomes exceedingly worthy of attention. This port, on account of its central situation between the two cities of Su-chew-fu and Hang-chew-fu and its proximity to the Yangs-cse-kiang, certainly combines many advantages.

is a port in Fo-kien.

I have also reason to think that the Porterage across these Mountains is more expensive on Tea than on other articles, owing to the inconvenient size of the package. It is more so than either silver or lead; and it is certain that the Woollens are unpacked at Canton and repacked into chests, which contain four or five pieces, in order to render the package more convenient for carriage. Again, the route by which Teas pass out of Fo-kien, is considered as difficult and expensive, and is not the usual one from the coast into Kiang-sy and Che-kiang. It is therefore not doubt dearer. Thus a further saving would be made in favor of Woollens. Until better information, however, be obtained upon these points, it would be useless to estimate the expense of transporting goods to the Principal Marts of Trade The advantage, or otherwise, will principally depend upon the navigation up the River Min, and the Passage across the Mountains.

The little information I possess upon this subject leads me to think that goods can be transported cheaper from Fu-chew-fu to Hang-chew-fu than from Canton to Hang-chew-fu; to Han-keu also a trifle less; but to Nan-chang-fu and the Green Tea Districts the expense would be rather more. But even supposing the expense of transporting Woollens from Fu-chew-fu to Hang-chew-fu to be the same as from Canton to Hang-chew-fu, which is quite improbable, still the bulk of the Woollens is so small compared with that of the Black Teas that the whole amount of Duties and Carriage of even five-sixths of the Woollens would not amount to so much as the carriage of Tea from the Vu-ye Mountains to the city of Hang-chew-fu, which is only half the distance, and Hang-chew-fu is the nearest Port to the Tea Districts, out of the Province of Fo-kien.

It is not to be supposed, however, that any reduction can be effected in the transport duties. The Chinese are unlikely to grant Privileges to foreigners which necessarily entail a loss on themselves; and if no saving be made in the duties, then the carriage of the same quantity of Woollens (five-sixths) would not amount to one-third of the carriage of Tea from Fo-kien. Again, the Tea Trade, though ostensibly a Trade of Barter, may really be considered a Trade in Cash. The advances made to the Tea Men are in dollars, not in Long-Ells; and the balance, though paid in Long-Ells, is converted as soon as possible into dollars and sent to Fo-kien. Thus, at any rate as far as the Province of Fo-kien is concerned, from the early advances until the final returns of the Tea, the Trade is a complete Cash transaction.

But if the Tea Men sell their Woollens for Cash, how much more advantageous must it be to the Company to do the same, and by sailing to Fo-kien with their dollars save the expense of transport on Tea. Still more certainly advantageous would it be to carry such dollars as we import to ourselves, or procure by bills, and these amount to no less than one-third of the Exports. It is obvious also that these arguments are applicable to any part from which the Tea Men are supposed to carry dollars to Fo-kien, whether it be from Canton, the Yang-cse-kiang, or the Gulph of Pe-chy-ly. That in an open Trade our Ships would resort to Fo-kien carrying dollars to prevent the inland transport of so bulky an article as Tea cannot be doubted; and since this is the natural state of the Trade, in an open and unrestrained intercourse with China, it is what under any circumstances is much to be desired. Such then is the importance of a Port in Fo-kien, on account of the great expense of crossing the mountains in the Province.

Kiang-nan. With respect to a Port in Kiang-nan, the advantages are all speculative; they depend upon nothing which is reducible to figures; they all turn on expected increased consumption of Imports, or increased price, or both, though as to what effect may be produced, either on price or consumption, I confess myself utterly ignorant. To me, it appears a subject in its nature too complex to speculate upon, even if we possessed more accurate and extensive information than we are ever likely to obtain in our present restrained and limited intercourse with this country. The only certainty distinctly to be seen is that as far as the Population, Wealth, Actual Consumption, and Easy Transport of Goods are concerned, a Port on the Yang-cse-kiang is the most favorable Geographical Situation for the introduction of all articles of general consumption. It is there where probably the most extensive consumption and highest prices may be maintained; but what that consumption or those prices may be is impossible to conjecture.

Both Ports are highly important to the interests of the Company, the one as it affects Consumption or Imports; the other, Production or Exports; and each may have its advocates. Those who delight to frame magnificent schemes of an unlimited Consumption of our Imports, converting at the same time the Woollens and all other unprofitable articles into profitable ones, will choose a Port in Kiang-nan. But those who are unwilling to sacrifice a certain Profit to speculative advantages will give the preference to the Port of Fu-chew-fu. I shall therefore now show the benefits that would result to the Company's interests from the opening of this Port.

Fu-chew-fu. The city of Fu-chew-fu is situated in Lat. 26°2', N. Long. 119°30' E. in the Province of Fo-kien. The distance from the city to the probable place of anchorage is about 30 miles (Horsburg says seven leagues), which is about the same distance as from Canton to the Second-Bar. By the Chart, the Port appears a favorable one, and contains a sufficient depth of water for the largest of the Company's Ships. Among other advantages which this city possesses is the important one of its being the residence not only of the Fu-yen but the Tsong-tu, or Viceroy, who presides over this Province and the adjacent one of Che-kiang.

The sudden removal of a trade of great magnitude from the channels in which it has been accustomed to flow is neither easy nor desirable. But never, perhaps, was a change of this nature proposed presenting fewer difficulties, or apparently less pregnant with risk or inconvenience than that of the removal of the export trade to the Port of Fu-chew-fu. It is the capital of the Province, and in the vicinity of the district where the principal Article of Export is grown and manufactured; it is in the native Province of the merchants or factors who bring this article to Canton, with whom of late years we have personally, in conjnction with the Hong merchants, entered into contracts, to whom we have annually made considerable advances of money, and who are consequently acquainted with our manners, customs, and mode of conducting business. A mutual confidence in and knowledge of each other's character and resources is therefore established; and these People who at present contract to bring their teas to Canton, with all the inconveniences of a tedious route -- partly mountainous -- suffering a long separation from their homes and families, would obviously prefer conveying them by the more natural and easy channels of Fu-chew-fu, where such inconveniences would be avoided and consequent deprivations greatly diminished; the necessary arrangements might be made with these People, and in one year the principal part of the Export Trade removed to that Port. The increased demand for Warehouses and Boats could form no impediment to such arrangements in a City so extensive and Populous as that of Fu-chew-fu.

But where the principal advantages of opening a new Port are expected to be derived from the Import Trade, it is equally evident the same facilities could not be afforded. Even if the Canton Hong merchants were to remove with their families to that part of the Empire, as was the case with the Fo-kien merchants when the intrigues and superior influence of the Canton Government occasioned the European Trade to be exclusively confined to that Port, still these People, though natives of China, would experience all the difficulties of new settlers in a strange Province and many years must elapse before that mistrust inseparable from all transactions with strangers could be surmounted and that confidence established which is necessary to render the Import Trade important to the Company's interest.

Supposing it to be desirable to retain a part of the Export Trade at Canton, the articles that can be brought to that City at least loss are the Green Teas, Raw Silk, and Nankeens. I shall therefore divide the Trade into two divisions, assigning to Canton the Exports of Green Tea, Raw Silk, and Nankeens, and Imports of the present quantity of Bombay Cotton, Lead, Iron, and Woollens for the consumption of all the Provinces of Fo-kien, Che-kiang, Kiang-nan, Shan-tong, Shan-sy, and Pe-chy-ly. The difference between Imports and Exports at the Port of

Fu-chew-fu might be supplied as at present by Bills on India and England, and the amount sent in Dollars from Canton in Ships that would sail from thence to that Port or rather by means arising out of that increase of India and British Trade which I shall presently shew would take place in Fo-kien in consequence of opening a Port in that Province.

The Tonnage necessary for the Exports from Canton being less than that required for the Imports could occasion no material loss or inconvenience, and might be productive of considerable advantage. New sources of Trade may be opened, and a Coasting Trade established, either on freight or otherwise. That such a Trade exists to a prodigious extent among the Chinese is evident from the numerous Fo-kien Junks in the Canton River, and the innumerable Trading Vessels daily passing to and fro at Macao, and along every part of the Coast of China. Doubtless in a free and open intercourse with this Country, the superior construction and security of European Vessels and knowledge of Insurance would enable Foreigners not only to participate in but perhaps monopolize this Branch of Commerce, and even attract to the Coast much of that still more valuable Trade which from the risks and fears of a Sea Voyage is at present conducted by inland carriage. A great part of the Trade between Manila and Macao is already carried on in Portuguese and Spanish Vessels, freighted by Chinese. But even supposing no better expedient could be devised than paying double Port Charges on ships that would sail empty from Canton to Fu-chew-fu, still the loss would not amount to Forty Thousand Tales.

Nor would the expense of a second establishment be great. The Trade at Canton would be comparatively small. The Imports would arrive between the months of July and September; and even allowing that any favorable circumstances occasioned by the removal of the Trade to Fo-kien should enable the Green Teas to be brought to Canton six weeks sooner than ordinary, still they could not be finally shipped before the first of January. Thus the length of time the ships must unavoidably remain at Canton, together with the smallness of the Trade, would enable the business of the Season to be managed by a few Persons.

Ships bound to Fu-chew-fu ought not to come up the China Seas after the middle of August, to insure a direct passage through the Straits of Formosa. At that Season of the year, ships sailing to Macao would make the Eastern part of the Macclesfield Bank. The course from thence to the parallel of Macao in a passage to Fu-chew-fu lies as much to the eastward of North as the course to Macao is westward of North -- say the one is NNE, and the other is NNW -- then, with a southerly wind, the time required to sail to that parallel would be the same in both cases, and the difference of passage from this parallel to Fu-chew-fu could not occupy more than two or three days, for the voyage from Macao to Fu-chew-fu has often been performed by ships in three or four days, which is nearly double the distance. The Black Teas would arrive at Fu-chew-fu from the months of September to November, so that the whole Fleet might be ready again for sea by the first of December. They consequently would arrive and sail at the finest season of the year; and as the whole Business of both Ports would be completed by the month of January, there would be a saving of time and consequently of expense.

I shall now estimate the saving that would arise on the Carriage of Black Tea to the Port of Fu-chew-fu. The Teas that go from Fo-kien to Canton are brought almost entirely by inland conveyance through the Province of Kiang-sy. The journey generally occupies forty days, and sometimes two months. The distance is about 750 miles, and the expense of transport, exclusive of duties, is three Tales, six Mace, and five Candareens per Pecul. Such as are brought by Sea, which are very few, * are transported down the River Min, and in eight days they arrive at the City of Fu-chew-fu. The distance from the Tea Districts to this City is about 240 miles; and the expense about four Mace, three Candareens per Pecul. The difference of expense therefore between these two routes would be three Tales, two Mace, a saving of fifteen per cent on the present cost of the Tea to the Chinese Hong Merchants at Canton. The exports of Black Tea being 152,374 Peculs, the saving in carriage alone would amount (at three Tales, two Mace per Pecul) to Tales 487,597, or £162,532 per annum. Such is the advantage of this Port.

There are, however, savings on other items, and those considerable, whose precise amount cannot be estimated, such as the Tea Men's personal expenses; those of their clerks and other attending the boats; loss of time and loss of comfort in being separated from their homes and families; the expense of transporting dollars from Canton to the amount at least of 2,500,000 per annum on the Company's Account alone; interest of money at a high rate; and damage of goods. All those expenses fall either directly or indirectly on the price of Tea and would be greatly diminished by the Company's dealing near the spot where the principal article of Export is grown and manufactured.

Besides these several savings on Tea, the great accession of Wealth that would accrue to Fu-chew-fu from its becoming an Emporium of the Trade would occasion throughout the Province of Fo-kien a considerable and almost immediate increased consumption of every article of European produce. Nor would this increase be a mere transfer of consumption from Canton; for however much the present prosperity of that part of the Empire may be ascribed to its long connection with the Foreign Trade, yet as it is simply the Emporium and not the Seat of consumption of more than one-sixth part of the Woollens, not the place of Growth or Manufacture of any of the Exports, it is exceedingly

* See below, p. 20

probable that the Trade has been principally important in determining a quantity of capital, talent, and domestic industry to the Province which is now altogether independent of Foreigners. New Manufactures may have risen up owing, indeed, their origin to the increased wealth of the Province derived from the Foreign Trade, but which have now taken too firm a root to be materially affected by its removal. Some diminution of consumption must take place, though not to the extent of the increase likely to be produced at Fu-chew-fu. The increase of the Trade, therefore, at a second Port would be real, and not merely a transfer of Consumption; and in whatever degree our Trade may have nursed and reared up new domestic Industry at Canton, the habits, the taste, and dispositions of the People being everywhere the same, similar effects would be produced at any Port to which the Trade may be removed. If some Articles of the Company's and Private Imports, such as Bombay Cotton, Lead, Iron, Tin, Beetle-nut &c., seem almost exclusively confined to Canton, it is not that this Province favors their consumption more than any other of the Empire, but merely from its being the only Port open to Europeans, and that such articles will not pay the expense of transport to other Provinces. Much of the Bengal Cotton is already manufactured in the Province of Fo-kien; and as the Bombay Cotton is principally employed in the manufacture of Cloths for the Poor and other inferior purposes, it is evidently equally suited to general consumption.

Fo-kien is a more favorable place than Canton for the introduction of Lead. I find by particular inquiry that the whole of the Lead of which the Tea Canisters for the Black Tea is made has for some years been procured from Han-keu in Hu-quong, not from any particular excellence of quality but because the expense of transport from Han-keu to the Tea Country is considerably less than from Canton. The cost at Han-keu to the Tea Country is considerably less than from Canton. The cost at Han-keu is about the same as that of the Company's Lead in the Country Market at Canton, and the expense of transport to the Tea Country is about One Tale, three Mace per Pecul. But the expense of transport from Fu-chew-fu would be only one tale per Pecul; consequently it might be procured cheaper from Fu-chew-fu than either from Canton or Han-keu. The quantity of Canisters annually made in the Tea Country may be estimated at 500,000, which at five Catties per Canister, would amount to 25,000 Peculs of Lead. The importation of 1814-15 amounted to less than 5,000 Peculs.

With respect to Iron, it is exceedingly doubtful whether unwrought iron ever can become an advantageous article of Import, though some articles of wrought iron may. If any Provinces favor its introduction it can only be such as have no Mines. But Canton is well supplied with Iron, and even Lead, from Mines in the immediate vicinity of the City. There does not then appear much reason to imagine that Iron would find a less favorable sale in the Province of Fo-kien than at Canton.

Tin, Beetle-nut, Rattans, and other articles of Strait's Produce already find a considerable consumption in Fo-kien, where they are carried by Junks or Vessels belonging to that Province. The remaining articles, as Opium, Woollens, Skins, Pearls, Beach de Mar, Birds' Nests, Spice, Pepper, and Sandal Wood, also find a Sale in Fo-kien; and these being articles capable of bearing the expense of transport to distant Provinces, Fu-chew-fu, from its proximity to the City of Hang-chew-fu and Province of Kiang-nan -- the great seat of Population and Wealth as well as the point of union of the Great Rivers and Canals of the Country -- is more favorably situated than Canton for the diffusion of these articles over the Empire.

Thus, as no additional expense would be incurred for the Carriage of Goods to any of the Principal Marts of Trade, the great saving will arise on the Black Teas, which has already been shewn to amount in boat hire alone to Tales 487,597, or £162,532 per Ann., to which must be added the other great savings of Tea before enumerated, the profits arising from increased consumption of Imports; and any saving that may be made in the transport of Woollens and other Goods to Hang-chew-fu, from which must be deducted the expense of a Second Establishment, and double Port Charges upon such ships as sail to two Ports. Supposing then the Port of Fu-chew-fu to be obtained, a saving would there ensue which is not attainable at any other Port in China; and whatever contingent advantages may render other Ports desirable, still these advantages can never lessen the importance of the Port of Fu-chew-fu.

The advantages also to be derived from the change here proposed are not remote and speculative, but immediate and real; and whatever errors may have entered into this investigation, feel fully confident that the result will be nearly the same, and most important in its consequences to the Company's and British Interests. Nor are the obstacles to the opening of a Second Port relatively to the Chinese of a nature insurmountable. Perhaps it might not be difficult to shew that a change would be mutually beneficial; and whatever may have been said of the Jealousy and Suspicion of these People, it may be doubted whether they are so bigoted to forms as to sacrifice even their smallest Interests where a Change seems to involve no radical injury to their Institutions. They have no objection to the Trade if it can be carried on peaceably; and nothing can appear more reasonable on our part, or more intelligible to them, than our wishing to carry it on where we can purchase the articles we require the cheapest. It is not, however, by intention to speculate upon this subject, but merely to elicit inquiry as to what Port would be the most beneficial to the Company's Interests, should we ever have it in our power to choose.

Objections to Ports Previously Named. Amoy is a most extensive and beautiful Port, so free from dangers that ships may sail in and out without Pilots. The principal danger is a rock at the entrace of the harbour. There is no River, however, of any magnitude in its immediate vicinity which communicates either with the Tea Country or the neighbouring Provinces. The Teas that are brought to Amoy are chiefly transported down the River Min to Fu-chew-fu, and are carried by Porters a great part of the way to Amoy. It consequently is a less favorable situation than Fu-chew-fu.

Ning-po is also an excellent harbour, but as the Teas must cross the Mountains of Fo-kien, either by the route of Csong-ngan or Pu-ching, it is obviously also a less favorable situation than Fu-chew-fu.

Of all Ports to the Northward, that of Chu-san has of late years been deemed the most advantageously situated for the Company's Trade. If preferred from any idea of security, it is not security of Person or Property that is meant, but security against Insult -- a kind of security that implies power of defense. But Power is surely the last privilege that a jealous and suspicious People are ever likely to grant to Foreigners. It may be wrested from them; so might a Settlement on the main, which would be still more advantageous, if there be any thing in a Settlement really desirable. Examine the Country to the Eastward of the Grand Canal in that part of Kiang-nan which lies between the City of Hang-chew-fu and the River Yang-cse-kiang; mark how it is intersected with Canals, Rivers, and Lakes: Would an Island be more defensible? Examine also the Land that lies between the River Min, near the City of Fu-chew-fu in Fo-kien, and an arm of the Sea to the Southward of the River. It is almost an Island. Observe the Islands at the mouth of the same River, and the peninsulated form of the land that projects into the Sea. If Chu-san be thought desirable purely on Commercial Principles, it evidently must be less so than Fu-chew-fu.

With respect to Formosa and Cochin-China it may be observed that whatever at present prevents the Teas being brought to Canton in Junks would form a similar impediment to any Port where the Chinese Junks or Vessels go by Sea; and if we would overcome this impediment, we must pay for it accordingly. If the Teas are in fact brought by land to Canton and not by Sea, it is obvious that when all the risks and fears are calculated, the Sea conveyance is more expensive.

WOOLLENS

It is not to be supposed that an accurate account can be given of the quantity of Woollens consumed in each Province. The annexed statements, however, furnished by different Persons mark a considerable coincidence and may be deemed a sufficiently near approximation to truth to answer all purposes of the present inquiry. The quantity Imported is somewhat exaggerated in the Account A, but not much, as it was grounded upon the Importations prior to Season 1814-15.

ACCOUNT A

	b. cloth	l. ells	camb.
Pe-chy-ly	1,000	4,000	300
Shen-sy			
Shan-sy	100	5,000	300
Shan-tong	700	5,000	300
Kiang-nan	5,000	40,000	8,100
Che-kiang	700	10,000	500
Fo-kien	700	5,000	500
Kiang-sy	400	30,000	1,000
Hu-pe or Han-keu*	500	50,000	1,000
Hu-nan*	300	10,000	1,000
Se-chuen	500	5,000	500
Quey-chew	100	3,000	100
Yun-nan	200	3,000	100
Quong-sy	100	4,000	300
Quong-tong	2,500	24,000	4,000
	12,800	198,000	18,000

ACCOUNT B+

	b. cloth	l. ells	camb.
Kiang-nan	8,000	40,000	10,000
Kiang-sy	800	40,000	10,000
Hu-pe or Han-keu*	1,000	50,000	1,000
Hu-nan*	500	10,000	500
Se-chuen	500	10,000	1,000
Quong-sy / Quong-tong	2,000	30,000	2,000
	12,800	180,000	24,500

* Hu-quong

\+ In the Account B it is observed that the whole of the Woollens are sent to the above-mentioned places, in the proportions there noticed, whence they are spread over the Empire, and that the remainder are consumed at Canton, which may be estimated as above.

The Woollens for Kiang-nan and Che-kiang in the preceding Accounts A and B pass by the route of Hang-chew-fu, where they are obliged to be landed and reshipped. Those for Kiang-nan proceed on to the City of

Su-chew-fu and are, I imagine, principally consumed in that City and in the neighbouring part of the Eastern division of Kiang-nan, north of Su-chew-fu and south of the Yang-cse-kiang. A few may find their way to the Northern Provinces, but not many. The quantity necessary for the supply of this District, which may be considered as connected with the trade of the Yang-cse-kiang, may be estimated at 35,000 pieces; leaving 15,000 pieces for Kiang-nan South of Su-chew-fu and the Province of Che-kiang, connected with the trade of Hang-chew-fu. The consumption of Long Ells in Kiang-sy cannot be estimated at more than from 10 to 15 thousand pieces. The surplus quantity in the Accounts A and B, must therefore be intended for the supply of the Western Division of Kiang-nan, the Eastern Division of the same Province north of the Yang-cse-kiang, Shan-tong, Shan-sy, and Pe-chy-ly. The expense of transport from Canton to Nan-chang-fu, being less than from Canton to Hang-chew-fu, accounts for the supply of these places proceeding by the former route.

Supposing then the Importation of Long Ells to be 180,000 pieces, the consumption of the under-mentioned places may be estimated as follows:

Shan-tong, Shan-sy, and Pe-chy-ly	20,000	or one-ninth *
Kiang-nan south of Su-chew-fu, Che-kiang, and Fo-kien	20,000	or one-ninth *
Canton and Quong-sy	30,000	or one-sixth *
Trade of the Yang-cse-kiang	110,000	or three-fifths *
Pieces	180,000	

Even admitting the consumption of Broad Cloth and Camblets to be in the same proportions, then in a Free Trade, supposing the Navigation to be favorable, these Districts would be supplied from Ports in the under-mentioned places; and the quantity and amount of Woollens imported into each of these Ports would be as follows:

Gulph of Pe-chy-ly+, for the supply of Shan-tong, Shan-sy, and Pe-chy-ly, one-ninth. . . . . Tales	270,552
Yang-cse-kiang, for the supply of Su-chew-fu, Nan-chang-fu, Han-keu, and Provinces connected with the Trade of these Marts, three-fifths, say	1,488,036
Hang-chew-fu, Kiang-nan south of Su-chew-fu, Che-kiang, and Fo-kien, one-ninth	270,552
Canton, for the supply of Canton and Quong-sy, one-sixth	405,828
Tales	2,434,968

* This estimate greatly exceeds the supposed consumption of the above places in the Accounts A and B.

\+ The Gulph of Pe-chy-ly seems to afford no shelter for large vessels. In that case, the supply of these Provinces would proceed from the Yang-cse-kiang, thus increasing the importance of that Port.

A d d superior Long Ells and other Woollens unaccounted for in the Accounts A and B 171,632

Total Tales 2,606,600

Observations of the Woollen Trade. It is erroneous to imagine that the Woollens cannot be sold by the Company for Cash at Canton without their sustaining a greater loss than is already experienced by the Hong Merchants and Tea Factors. It rarely happens that any of the Hong Merchants send their Woollens to the distant Provinces; and still more so for the Tea Men to traffic in these articles. It is true that the latter receive them partly in exchange for Tea; but they sell them again to the Shopkeepers, or Drapers, at Canton for the market price of the day and receive new or unstamped Dollars in return, which they carry to Fo-kien. No Woollens are sent into Fo-kien by the route common to the Tea Men; they all pass either by sea or along the southern and eastern coast of the Provinces of Quong-long and Fo-kien. It may be true that the wealthy Hong Merchants occasionally find an advantage in keeping their Woollens for a time, but it is clear that when the supply of an article is regular, or at least unlikely to be diminished, that not much is to be done by keeping. Those who have kept Woollens have sometimes lost and sometimes gained, like all other speculators, and I fear more frequently the former than the latter. It cannot be doubted when the supply exceeds the demand that the prices will be lowered; but it depends upon this one circumstance, and no other: at any rate, not upon a large quantity being sold in a short space of time. Teas are not bought cheaper by Europeans because they are all brought down about the same time. Those who buy are fully as eager as those who sell. Both parties have an interest in returning to their homes before a certain time. It must also be observed that Canton is the mere Emporium of the Trade; the Canton people are neither the carriers of the Imports to the distant Provinces nor of the Exports to Canton. It consequently is frequented by Merchants of all descriptions from the very extremities of the Empire, and is supposed to receive more Strangers (Ke) during the season of Trade than any other Province. Those from Fo-kien, Kiang-nan, and Hu-quong exceed all others in number. These Merchants arrive during the months of November and December and by the month of April or May scarcely any, except a few of the Black Tea Men or their Agents remain. It is therefore as much the interest of the People who purchase the Cloths to return to the Markets where they hope to effect a resale of their purchases, as for the Tea Men to return to Fo-kien in time to renew their purchases of the Tea. It may also be observed that these Persons have no kind of intercourse with each other, but both deal with intermediate People, the Cloth Men or Drapers, whose shops are innumerable in every part of the suburbs of Canton. There is therefore little reason to apprehend a combination amoung the Country Merchants, or Drapers, at

Canton, but under any circumstances the Company would not obtain worse terms than the Tea Men; and it is unnecessary to add, if the Tea Men lose by their Woollens, they must charge more for their Tea.

Imports. The quantity and amount of goods imported in season 1814-1815, were as follows:

	Pieces	Amount of Invoice Tales		Tales
broad cloth	8,592	768,976	loss	50,796
long ells	179,510	1,438,640	"	93,378
superior long ells	11,780	130,065	"	18,369
embossed long ells	800	8,014	gain	765
camblets	26,600	495,823	loss	64,197
worleys	3,940	50,619	gain	528
iron	3,447,300	75,439	loss	12,266
lead	559,961	28,016	"	9,409
Bombay cotton, pls.	42,413	421,661	gain	112,139
	Invoice Amount		Tales	3,357,153 *
	Deduct loss			104,673 *
			Total	3,252,480

Exports. The following estimate makes the annual Exports of Tea Peculs 189,634, Tales 4,895,810. This estimate is grounded on the supposition that the annual consumption amounts to lbs. 24,000,000, and that the quantity shipped is no more than the quantity sold, with the exception of an allowance of five per cent for loss of weight and waste, which is supposing that neither sea loss nor damage takes place. The actual quantity shipped per annum may therefore be considered as somewhat greater.

Black Tea	Chests	Catts.	Peculs	Tales
Bohea	--	--	7,767	108,738
Congou, packed in Bohea chests	--	--	3,107	49,742
Winter Souchong, ind. Cong.	8,000	55	4,400	96,800
Ditto Congou	45,154	65	29,350	587,080
Ditto Campoi	6,200	55	3,410	88,660
Contract Congou	145,000	65	94,250	2,544,750
Ditto Souchong	2,000	55	1,100	44,000
Add 5 per cent for waste,			143,384	3,519,660
&c., on Peculs 180,600			9,000	243,000
			152,384	3,762,660

(chart continued on following page)

* Discrepancy in original [ed.]

Green Tea.				
Twankay	45,000	61	27,450	741,150
Hyson Skin	10,000	49	4,900	132,300
Hyson	10,000	49	4,900	259,700
			37,250	1,133,150
Total weight and amount of B. & G. Teas			189,634	4,895,810

The Exports will therefore be as follows:

Black Tea.	152,384*	3,762,660	from Fo-kien
Green Tea	37,250*	1,133,150	from
Raw Silk.	1,556	507,483	Kiang-nan &
Nankeens . . . . . . Pieces	179,000	118,390	Che-kiang
	Tales	5,521,683	

* The actual quantity of Teas shipped at Canton, on the Company's Account, from season 1810-11 to 1814-15, both inclusive, gives an average annual quantity of:

Black Tea.	Peculs	161,217	Tales	4,087,794
Green Tea	"	35,862	"	1,082,662
	Peculs	197,079	Tales	5,170,456

The Mountainous Passes in Fo-Kien. The lofty mountains that encompass the Province of Fo-kien on every side towards the main seem to isolate it as it were from the rest of the Empire; and perhaps the difficulties of communication by land, added to the natural sterility of the soil and mountainous aspect of the Country, may have tended in some degree to create that superior hardihood and adventurous spirit which the People of the Province are said to possess over the other Inhabitants of the Coast and which renders them the great carriers by sea of the produce of the neighbouring Provinces, as well as the principal traders to Japan, Formosa, Manila, and the Eastern Isles. The greater part of the large Junks that visit the Port of Canton, even those from Tien-sing in Pe-chy-ly, are said to belong to Fo-kien. It is also worthy of remark that the principal Cities of Fo-kien are chiefly maritime Cities.

Pass of Fun-shuey-kuon, near Csong-ngan-hien. The journey from Csong-ngan in Fo-kien into Kiang-sy is amidst a range of stupendous mountains varying in their height and form, some consisting of huge masses of black rock while others are covered to their very summits with the Camphor, the Larch, and other lofty trees. During the whole of this journey scarcely a spot of cultivation or a fixed habitation is seen. Temporary sheds are erected in some of the deep valleys for the convenience of the Porters, where they sleep and obtain refreshment at the end of each day's stage, but these buildings are said to be removed as soon as the transport of the Teas is completed. Two more convenient and permanent habitations or Inns are erected, however, at a day's journey from each other for the use of the Tea Merchants, who usually pass in their light Bamboo Sedan Chairs in three days from Csong-ngan-hien to Ho-keu, though the Porters are generally from eight to ten days carrying the Teas from Csong-ngan-hien to the stream which takes its rise at the foot of the mountains near Yuen-shan-hien, which is a shorter distance. The Road, which is rudely paved with small square stones, sometimes winds round the base of a lofty mountain, then rising half way up the acclivity of another, sinks again into the deep valleys below. In many different places it lies across the shallow stream that encircles these mountains in every direction, over which the Teas are sometimes ferried, and sometimes carried across wooden bridges, which extend a considerable distance on either side of the stream to prevent their being washed away during the rains when the torrents from the mountains suddenly swell this shallow stream to the size of a large river.

Pass of San-kuon, near Shau-u-fu. The Pass near the City of Shau-u-fu, or Xaou-chew-fu, appears a much frequented route, and I imagine the direct one from Fu-chew-fu into Kiang-sy. This City forms one of the Keys to the Province, and stands on the West bank of the river Czu in Lat. 27 25' N Long. 117 50' E. This river takes its rise in the chain of the mountains that divides the Province of Fo-kien from that of Kiang-sy, situated to the NW of the city, and glides from thence first southward and then eastward by the City of Shau-u-fu. Then serpentining in its course to the southward, it falls into the River Si near the town of Ciang-lo, whence taking first an easterly and then a southerly direction, after receiving the waters of the Si-ki, flows past the City of Yen-ping-fu and finally discharges the united waters of these rivers into the river Min. On the western side of the same mountains whence the river Czu takes its rise near the pass of San-kuon is a river in the Province of Kiang-sy, which flowing in a direction to the NW passes the two Cities of Kyen-chang-fu and Fu-chew-fu and falls into the Han-kiang between the two Cities of Nan-chang-fu and Lin-kyang-fu.

Pass near Pu-ching-hien. The mountains near the Pass of Pu-ching-hien, which lie in the direct route from Fu-chew-fu to Hang-chew-fu, are described by Du Halde as "being very steep and the valleys very deep. They have made this road as even as the nature of the ground will permit; it is paved with square stones and furnished with towns full of Inns for lodging Travellers. On one of these mountains they have made stairs consisting of more than three hundred steps of flat stones which go winding round it to render the ascent more easy. This road begins near the town of Pu-ching-hien, and continues for near thirty leagues together to Kiang-shan-hien. No less than ten thousand Porters are here employed in carrying Goods to and from the Province of Che-kiang." I have no acquaintance with this Pass, but it is evident from the number of Towns, Inns, and Porters here spoken of that this route must be a much frequented one, and that considerable traffic exists on the River Min to and from the Province of Fo-kien.

Transport of the Black Tea to Canton.

Island Transport. Almost the whole of the Black Tea is transported by inland carriage to Canton. It is first collected and packed at the town of Sing-csun, situated amidst the mountains of Vu-ye, and from thence conveyed to Csong-ngan-hien upon rafts, each carrying twelve chests. It is then carried by Porters across a mountainous and expensive route to Yuen-shan-hien, which journey occupies upon an average eight days. From this place, it is transported to Ho-keu, in small boats which hold about twenty-two chests. At Ho-keu it is landed and transshipped into larger boats which convey it to Kan-chew-fu. These boats are said to carry about two hundred chests; but in approaching the City of Ky-ngan-fu, the waters are frequently very shallow, a circumstance which not only occasions a detention to the Tea on its passage but the transshipment of a certain quantity into smaller boats, to enable the larger ones to pass over the shallows. A similar inconvenience also prevails near the sources of the two rivers Kan-kiang and Pe-kiang, on either side of the mountains which divide the two Provinces of Kiang-sy and Quong-tong. * In passing the She-pa-tan, which are torrents formed by rocks lying across the bed of the river, some skill is required to prevent ship wreck. Men accustomed to the navigation are therefore hired as Pilots for this purpose; and it is here where the principal damage on Tea takes place in its transport to Canton. From Kau-chew-fu it is conveyed to Nan-gan-fu in boats which carry about sixty chests, where it is again landed and carried by Porters over the great mountain of Ta-Moey-lin to Nan-hyong-fu, in the Province of Quong-tong. On their arrival at Nan-hyong-fu, the Tea is again shipped, and carried to Shau-chew-fu, where it is transshipped into larger boats which carry from five to eight hundred chests, and thus conveyed to Canton. The whole expense of Carriage from the Black Tea Country to Canton may generally be estimated at Three Tales, Six Mace per Pecul. The charge of Boat hire varies as the traffic on the rivers is much or little.

Traffic by Sea. When the Teas are brought by Sea to Canton, "they

* Mr. Barrow thus speaks of the river near Nan-gan-fu, "At Nan-gan-fu the river Kan-kiang ceases to be navigable. Indeed the whole of the three last days' navigation might with propriety in England be called only a trout stream; upon which no nation on earth, except the Chinese, would have conceived the idea of floating any kind of craft; they have, however, adapted, in an admirable manner, the form and construction of their vessels to the nature and depth of the navigation. Yet, in several places, the water was so shallow that they could not be dragged over, until a channel had been made, by removing the stones and gravel with iron rakes."

are shipped at Sing-csun, a town situated in the Bohea Country, each boat carrying about fifty chests. In one day they arrive at Vu-ye-ho-keu, where they are then transshipped into larger boats each carrying two hundred chests. They are then transported down the river Min to Fu-chew-fu. In the Spring when the currents are rapid, in four days they arrive at Fu-chew-fu, but in Autumn it requires eight. They are then shipped in Junks, which carry five or six thousand chests each, and in fourteen or fifteen days they arrive at Canton.

Now when the transshipments of the Tea, the carriage by Porters the length of time, and other inconveniences of the inner passage are considered, it requires very little illustration to prove that in a good state of navigation, the transport by Sea would be a considerable saving. Some of the Chinese reckon it a half, and none less than a third, when the junks are successful in their passage; but the risks from Pirates, the bad construction of their Vessels, ignorance of Insurance, and perhaps a natural timidity of Character, added to an aversion to the Sea, present such difficulties to the minds of these People that few Persons, and these principally adventurers, give the passage by Sea a preference.

It is therefore difficult to ascertain with much precision the expense of transport from the Bohea Country to Fu-chew-fu.

	m.	c.
One person reckons it from Sing-csun to Kien-ning-fu	1	2
and from Kien-ning-fu to Fu-chew-fu, ...	2	0
making the whole Expense of Carriage	3	2

Another makes it only 40/100 of a Dollar, or 2 Mace, 8 Candareens, 8 Cash per Pecul; but a third, 6 Mace, 8 Candareens. I am inclined to think the two first accounts most deserving of credit; but we will take the mean, and reckon it 4 Mace, 3 Candareens per Pecul.

	t.	m.	c.	c.
Thus the inland Carriage to Canton, exclusive of duties, being per Pecul	3	6	5	0
and the Carriage to Fu-chew-fu only	0	4	3	0
the saving on Carriage would amount to per Pecul	3	2	2	0
<u>Expense of Packing.</u>				
Sing-csun, Hong Master, every two Chests. . . .	0	2	2	4
ditto Expenses,.	0	1	0	0
Quarter Chests,.	0	3	6	0
Paper Covering to Chests,.	0	0	4	6
Canisters,.	0	4	0	0
Expense of Packing, ...	0	0	9	0

	t.	m.	c.	c.
Expense of Bamboo Mats	0	0	5	0
Ditto Writing the Chop name on the Mats	0	0	2	0
Ditto Rope	0	0	2	6
	1	3	1	6

The River Min.

The only navigable River of importance in the Province of Fo-kien is the River Min, one of the branches of which divides itself into several small streams that flow in and about the mountains of Wu-i, the Country in which the Black Tea is produced. To the southward of these mountains, at the town of Chien-yang hsien, these several streams unite and then flow in a SE direction to Chien-ning fu. This is a City of much trade, as it lies in the way of all Goods that pass up and down the river to and from the Provinces of Che-kiang and Kiang-nan, and upon a census taken in 1790 was found to contain a Population of about 260,000 inhabitants. * This branch of the river begins to be navigable at the town of Chung-an-hien, situated about ten miles to the NE of Chin-ning-fu. About ten miles to the north of this latter City these two branches unite, and then flowing for about forty miles in a direction nearly south pass the City of Yen-ping-fu. Here, after receiving the waters of three other rivers, the Czu, the Sy, and the Sy-kee, whose sources lie in the SW part of the Province, the river then takes a course nearly SE and flows into the Sea about 30 miles below the City of Fu-chew-fu, the capital of the Province. Its distance from Yen-ping-fu is about 110 miles, making the whole course of the river from the towns of Csong-ngan-hien and Pu-ching-hien about 270 miles. Ogilby observes that "from the town of Pu-ching-hien to Kiu-keu, the river falls with great force of water, through valleys, rocks, and cliffs; but from thence glides on but slowly. In three days they go from the above town to Fu-chew-fu, with the stream, whereas they are fifteen days towing up against it." The Dutch Embassy under Van Hoorn in 1667, which passed up this river in the month of February on their way to Peking, were (exclusive of stoppages at certain towns) about seventeen days on their Passage from Fu-chew-fu to Pu-ching-hien, and seven days on their return in the months of September and November.

Fu-chew-fu, the Capital of the Province of Fo-kien.

This City presides over nine Cities of the third order. Besides the Fu-yen, the Tsong-tû, who is the Governor-General both of this Province and that of Che-kiang, resides here. It is famous for the advantage of its Situation, the greatness of its Trade, multitude of

* This account of the population of Kien-ning-fu is taken from a Chinese Statisical Work of recent publication.

its Literati, fertility of its Soil, beauty of its River, which carries the largest barks in the Empire up to the Walls, and lastly, for its admirable Bridge of above a hundred arches, built with fair white stone, across the bay. All its little hills are full of Cedars, Orange, and Lemon Trees."* This Port appears to be known to the English by the name of Ting-hai Harbor, from its circumstance of the Canton having been piloted here by a fisherman, 7th August, 1797. Horsbug observes, "she anchored in seven and a half fathoms of blue mud opposite the town, entirely surrounded by land. To the westward of this harbour, is a deep and extensive bay, formed by the two points of Ting-hay and May-how-sou." The same Author observes that "the River Chang+ falls into the bottom of this bay, and about seven leagues up stands the City of Fu-chew-fu; at the entrance of the river there are several islands and banks separated by narrow Channels from each other, and a little inside these banks is six or seven fathoms water."

Port in Kiang-nan.

It is doubtful whether Ships of heavy burthen can enter the river Yang-cse-kiang. This Port is thus described by Du Halde: "The breadth and depth of the Yang-cse-kiang rendered Nan-king formerly an excellent Port. The famous Corsair who besieged it in the late troubles passed easily up to it; but at present, the great barks, or rather the Chinese vessels of Carriage, do not enter the River, either because the mouth is stopped up of itself, or that the Chinese, out of policy, make no more use of it, that the knowledge of it by degrees may be lost." It is certain, however, that much of the Kiang-nan Cotton brought inland to the Southern Provinces is carried up the Yang-cse-kiang in junks. It is shipped at the town of Tong-chew, situated at the mouth of the Yang-cse-kiang, and is carried up that river as far as Kyeu-kiang-fu, in the Province of Kiang-sy, where it is transshipped into vessels of smaller size and conveyed to Canton. Similar doubts are also expressed by the same author respecting the entrance of the River Cien-tang-kiang which flows past the City of Hang-chew-fu, the Capital of Che-kiang: "The River opposite the City is about 4,000 Geometrical paces in breadth, but Ships cannot enter it because of its shallows." Supposing neither of these rivers to be accessible to Ships of heavy burden, the Port of Shang-hay-hien, near the City of Song-kiang-fu, should be surveyed. The same author gives the following description of these places: "The City of Song-kiang-fu is built in the water, and the Chinese Ships, or rather vessels of carriage, enter it on every side and so pass to the sea, which is not far

* Du Halde

\+ The name of this river is Min, not Chang. Chang I imagine to be a corruption of the word Kiang or Chiang, which in the Chinese Language signifies a River.

distant. The extraordinary quantity of Cotton and lovely Calicos of all sorts, wherewith it furnishes not only the Empire but also foreign Countires, render it famous and of very great resort. It has but four Cities under its jurisdiction, but it is neither the less fertile nor rich on that score, for though these Cities are of the third order, they may compare with the best for magnitude, the extraordinary resort of Merchants from all parts throughout the year, and the different sorts of Commerce carried on there. Such is for instance the Town of Shang-hay-hien, where ships from Fo-kien are continually entering, and others sailing out to trade with Japan." This town is placed by Du Halde in Lat. 31° 9' N but other authorities place it in 30° 14' and 16".

The importance, however, of Shang-hay-hien as a Port of Trade must depend upon the City of Su-chew-fu to enable a Factory to be established in that City and any sacrifice of Geographical position be deemed advisable to insure the residence of a Viceroy at the Port of Trade, then Su-chew-fu, from possessing this among other important advantages, would perhaps be the most eligible situation in all China for the Import Trade.

A DISSERTATION UPON THE COMMERCE OF CHINA

Anon., Canton, 1838

Trade is not here confined to one class of men, but to all ranks and ages. Scarcely can a boy lisp when he begins to sell a few cakes or a little sugar cane. The poorest try to gain a subsistence if it only were to dispose of a few rags. There is nothing in all nature which a Chinaman might not turn to advantage and trade in it. All recesses are ransacked to find a few trifles which may be sold to advantage, and he would rather procure a pittance in this way than receive the money without displaying his inventive genius. The more wealthy classes absorb their very existence in trade. Commerce is the invariable topic of conversation, the most important pursuit, the highest object of pleasure, and the very goal of all their wishes. Trade is the first and last word in which all unanimously join, whilst the energies of mind and body are consumed in following up this bent. Perhaps, the Jews excepted, no nation is so much influenced by the love of gain and at the same time so utterly regardless about the means to obtain this end. The government, though in theory discarding this trafficking spirit as mean and grovelling, and apparently discountenancing commerce as much as it encourages agriculture, is itself addicted to the general habit, and carries on a lucrative trade in selling justice and offices.

A Chinaman is energetic and persevering, and seldom daunted by failure. For the sake of a small profit he will venture very much, yea, put his life in jeopardy to realize it. Yet born under despotism, accustomed to see the Mandarin with the eagerness of a Tiger waiting for his prey, cunning and craftiness become a second nature, and are invariably transferred to commercial dealings. So deeply is this evil rooted in the Chinese breast, that even where straightforwardness in his transactions would be advantageous, he chooses the crooked paths as more congenial to his customary practice. Great is the scope which his love of adventure finds in his country and it is by no means extraordinary that all the resources which the land affords and the advantages arising from the Empire being civilized for many centuries, are put into requisition to save for the great purposes of commerce.

Productions. The produce of the country is doubtless as varied as that of any other state under similar circumstances. Still it might be increased if the Chinese were not too much wedded to antiquated custom. Grain being the staff of life, the utmost care is bestowed upon its cultivation, and often to the great injury of other equally useful herbs. It is the general received opinion that wherever grain will grow it should be planted, whilst less productive land may be assigned to other vegetables. Hence arises the want of variety in esculent roots and other vegetables for the use of men. Fruit trees as well as those of the forest are neglected, meadows are scarcely known, and pleasure grounds and parks are very seldom met with. But every article which constitutes a necessary of life is carefully extracted from the ground. In relation to the animal kingdom the Chinese are very sparing and cautious not to keep too many quadrupeds lest the food of man might be consumed by beasts. The pig makes an exception, because it is a very prolific animal, and can be fattened upon garbage. Cotton being adapted for all ordinary clothing, no great pains are bestowed upon rearing sheep, which nevertheless thrive very well in the Northern Provinces. But this neglect is amply compensated by the increased attention paid to the silk worm, in which we believe the Chinese are able to become teachers to the French and Italians.

Manufacture. A well grounded fear of government, lest the industry of the people might be withdrawn from the useful pursuits of agriculture and directed to digging after metals, has always prevented mining upon a large scale; but still there are extensive districts in Yunnan and Kueichoo and also in the Western Provinces where minerals are sought after. Iron is common throughout the Empire; there are also large coal mines. In the statistics we observe that silver ore is not found in as many places as gold; the latter is also procured from the sand of the Yang-tsze keang. Copper is scarce and mostly brought from Yunnan. Tin and lead are by far not sufficient for the Consumption. There is another article next in importance to grain, and this is salt. In the manufacture and transportation of the indispensable necessary are more people employed than in any other branch of trade.

Manufactures. The manufacturing industry of China, though still in its primitive simplicity, is not only equal to the home consumption but supplies also the adjacent countries. Silk, stuffs, and cotton goods made in China constitute the principal articles of export to Japan, Korea, Mongolia, and the western tribes. For the manufacture of useful things which constitute the necessaries of life the Chinese excell. They make them durable and suit them to the demand; but with the exception of silks, embroidery, lackered ware, and porcelain, they fabricate few costly articles to serve the purposes of luxury. For many centuries, however, they have been stationary and no new discovery had given impulse to their manufacturing industry. Though the inhabitants of Canton have learned important improvements from foreigners, yet these are confined to that district. In addition to the apathy with which the natives view the progress in every art and science, the Government is opposed to innovations and with a powerful arm upholds old customs. The nankeens and silks which are now in vogue were worn in the same manner five hundred years ago. Though their manufactures have thereby been thrown into the shade and can no longer compete with those of Europe, yet has the consumption amongst the neighboring tribes by no means decreased.

Currency. The introduction of coin is like every other thing in this country of an early date. Even amongst the cash of the present day one may pick out pieces cast 800 or 1000 years ago. The principle which guided the Chinese Government in issuing a circulatory medium was that of the utmost parsimony joined to durability. The bulk of the nation must under existing circumstances remain poor, hence the money ought to be adapted to their necessities and each piece of the smallest possible value. Cash was accordingly manufactured and the value of each dollar thus divided into one thousand parts. To that the most trifling sum might be accurately discharged and even the poorest secure a small quantity of coin. The precious metals being not in very great abundance, it was not advisable to follow a similar plan. The Government entirely abstained from coining silver, and left it to private individuals to cast it in lumps provided with a stamp of the silversmith to prove its being without alloy. The silver most current is entirely pure and contains often one percent of gold. Bullion of inferior description is undervalued, and in most transactions there is some difficulty in letting it pass. The benefit conferred by foreigners upon this country by importing dollars is incalculable. In all the great emporiums they are the common coin of the merchants, and though deformed and cut to pieces by stamping them, still they are considered more convenient than the sycee silver. Even the Government is persuaded of their great utility and has promoted their currency in the Provinces of the interior and lately issued a coin in imitation of them. Notwithstanding the great drain by exportation of no less than about 10 millions per annum, and the large sums which have been cast into lumps, yet the quantity still in circulation appears almost inexhaustible, though only small sums are at present imported. Gold cast in bars valuing from 180 to 220 dollars of various degrees of fineness but seldom under 80 touch or beaten into leaves is in use to a considerable extent, though more for the sake of hoarding up large sums in a small bulk and transporting them with ease than to facilitate commerce. The Government has not yet been able to succeed in substituting a paper currency for specie, because it is unwilling to redeem its pledge, and to receive its own issues back, but private capitalists have been more fortunate.

In most large trading towns are great banking establishments which issue notes. Their use, however, seldom extends beyond the limit of the respective cities. The system of drawing bills of exchange is still in its infancy and from the little credit which the cunning Chinese give to each other, subject to great inconveniences. This is a great hindrance to extensive dealings and a bar to commercial improvements most keenly felt by all wise merchants. Equally burdensome and destructive of free intercourse is the capacity of the magistrates to rob rich merchants. May a man be ever so innocent it is a crime to be rich and he must either give part of his gains to the local mandarins or allow himself to be pilfered at their pleasure to escape this dilemma. Rich houses invariably maintain an official agent at the head quarters of Government and pay largely and regularly for the immunities they enjoy. Many capitalists for fear of attracting notice keep their hoards buried and thus inflict a great injury upon commerce by withholding the disposable treasure. There is too little faith between the merchants who are always apprehensive of being overreached and they are on that account naturally backward in giving credits and thus hamper commercial dealings. The high rate of interest, from 10-30 percent, is another evil which considerably embarrasses trade, and renders bankrupts of frequent occurrence. Such disadvantages can only be remedied by a high degree of civilisation, and the general adoption of the principle that honesty is the best policy, a state of things which cannot soon be anticipated in China.

COMMERCIAL RELATIONS

Facilities and Restrictions. Though the Chinese are far behind us in commercial policy, they are on the other hand less subject to artificial systems, and there is either entire freedom of commerce with scarcely any important restrictions or a total prohibition, productive of extensive smuggling. We shall dwell upon these subjects more fully under the head of Government regulations, and here only allude so far to them as they affect the foreign and inland trade.

The liberal spirit of the Mantchoo rulers has made the rivers of the country and the High Seas free. Every citizen may embark in any branch of commerce he chooses, which is not in direct violation of the laws. Unfortunately it happens that the Custom house officers are here like in every other country very annoying and more careful about their own interests than those of their employers. To evade their oppression and elude their prohibitory regulations is the steady endeavour of every Chinese merchant, and smuggling is the very soul of their commerce. To meet this lawless tendency the Court has issued laws calculated to answer every exigency, which are a dead letter so long as they jar with the interests of the Collectors. Nowhere is smuggling so well organized and so much connived at with indifference as in China. Comparing the receipts of the customs with the consumption, scarcely a tenth part of the merchandise pays regular duties. Not only underlings but the highest dignitaries, even the officers of the imperial household themselves, sell licenses for this purpose or engage personally in illicit traffic. For anybody but a Chinaman such things when compared with the severe prohibitions on record may appear incredible, but in the country itself they are of so frequent occurrence as scarcely to elicit any remark.

Such a state of things has given to the Chinese dealer a cunning which would be very disgraceful to respectable merchants of other countries. Trade instead of being restricted by prohibitions, if yielding profit, flows only into a more rapid channel, as if there were no regulations to retard its progress. Waiving the fees which ought regularly to be paid, and some momentary interruption owing to misunderstanding or some new edicts, commerce may be considered in China as unshackled as anywhere in America and England. To this the country is in a great measure owing its prosperity.

Some drawback upon these facilities may be discovered in the monopolizing companies, whether established by Government itself or by a body of merchants of their own accord. This subject will claim further notice in the following pages. Here we merely speak about the combinations of the people, who on certain occasions declare their resolution not to trade if either the Government or any other body of men with whom they are at variance refuse certain concessions. This spirit of radicalism resembling our strikes manifests itself frequently, and though productive of a temporary stoppage of trade, brings the opposing party generally to terms.

The balance of trade, formerly a thing unknown, has only lately disturbed some Chinese statesmen, and their anxiety to maintain it confines itself to foreign commerce and does not affect the intercourse between the different provinces, as was the case in Germany. The scarcity of bullion very severely felt in the Imperial treasury first gave rise to the suspicion that foreign trade was detrimental because the country lost thereby great quantities of silver, especially by the purchase of the deleterious opium, and the alarms entertained by the ministry have of late considerably increased. But all the fanciful theories which marked the continental system of Europe under Napoleon have happily never entered the heads of the Chinese ministry and afflicted the country.

After these preliminary remarks we shall enter upon detailing the commercial relations of this country both of its inland as well as foreign trade, and endeavor to give as faithful a description as out scanty resources will permit.

Canton. We commence with Canton as the place best known to foreigners, which including the foreign commerce may on an aggregate be considered as the most flourishing commercial town in China. Its native commerce is certainly inferior to that of several other places, though it is impossible to form a true estimate, our only guide is the receipt of customs, which are very minutely published in a statistical work.

The Government, well aware that a wealthy mercantile community must always be very powerful and able to oppose its measures, removed the seat of an extensive commerce to the most distant part of the Empire to render its influence upon politics harmless. Foreigners moreover who repaired to China by combining with native merchants might often have turned the scale against the Rulers and rendered their power nugatory if they had been permitted to visit a port as near to the Capital as Tien-tsin; thus the maxim to remove them as far as possible from Peking and to keep them by every means possible at a distance operated strongly in favor of Canton, which was considered the most eligible spot to which they ought to be confined. Hence the commercial privileges granted to this city were ample and every inducement was held out to attract here as many merchants as could find employ for their capital and enterprise. It therefore became a mart for all commercial nations and merchants of every part of the Empire, superior in the extensiveness of its dealings to every other city in Asia.

Taking the numerous boats which constantly crowd the river as a criterion, the immense number of which fills every foreigner with astonishment, the inland trade must be very considerable. The importation of rice, sugar, and other raw produce from the larger cities and fertile districts to the Metropolis is very considerable. There exists a very lively commerce with the regions that border on Tonkin, from whence tropical productions, and especially areca and coca nuts, are imported in great quantities. The country around Canton being destitute of Timber, large rafts are floated down the river and in fact every article produced in the province which yields a profitable return is sure to reach this city.

Manufactures of Canton. In exchange for these goods, Canton gives home manufactures and importations from the foreign market. Its cotton manufactures which employ thousands of hands are everywhere in great demand, and though the natives cannot furnish a stuff equal in value and durability to the Nankeen of Keangsoo, they manufacture various other textiles which are peculiar to this place. These being very cheap find a ready sale. The intercourse which the Cantonese have had for so many years with foreigners has given them a decided superiority over their countrymen, which they have improved to their advantage. Thus they have learned to imitate several of our manufactures and furnish them at a much lower rate than other cities can afford. Though their durability thereby has not been the gainer, they are showy and easily attract customers. With all the disadvantages of manual labour and the primeval construction of looms and other implements, the Cantonese on account of the low wages and the persevering industry of the workmen can compete with us in the cheapness of several articles. Many of the most skillful men do not earn a guinea per month, the most industrious manufacturers get only three dollars on an average, and with this pittance, they are as content as if they earned as many pounds. A little rice and salt vegetables is their daily food, which they eat without grumbling. They keep no festival except the new year, and work from the early morning till late at night. Many labour on their own account and sell their woof as soon as it is ready, whilst the large manufacturing establishments are very few, comparatively.

In silk piece goods the people of Canton are still very inferior to the manufacturers of Keangsoo and Chekeang, and their raw silk which is made in the province is likewise of less value. These establishments are by no means of a very old date. Plenty of capital brought in circulation by the foreign trade and a constant demand for these articles prevail upon them to attempt entering into competition with their northern countrymen. Though they cannot equal the quality, they can sell cheaper and dispose of their goods to foreigners and the inhabitants of the Southern Provinces. Cotton they can obtain at a lower rate than the manufacturers of any other city, on account of the constant importation from India. With silk it is different for they can never rear the worm as well and as cheap as the inhabitants of Chekeang and ought therefore rest contented with emulating them without ever hoping to surpass them.

Lackered wares, which occupy the next place, are made in much smaller quantities for foreign parts than for the consumption of the various Provinces. To these whole boat loads of the cheapest description are annually sent.

China ware, once such an important article for the foreign market, had ceased, with the exception of the coarsest kind, to be any longer in demand in Europe. When the trade in porcelain flourished most, the goods were ordered in Keangse; since that, the Cantonese have become equally as expert in making cups and saucers as their rivals. The manufactures at Canton are very extensive and supply Southern China and other parts with this commodity.

Nowhere in the Empire are such extensive establishments for lapidaries as here. They cut all kinds of precious stones, including the cornolian, agate, topaz, &c., work in pearls, and make beads and other trinkets, especially bracelets to a very large extent. The amount of these manufactured articles is annually several millions in dollars. In this branch also the natives excel so much that they have almost monopolized it. Another extensive branch of industry are the glass manufactures; what they produce is very inferior to ours, but is recommended by its cheapness. Canton glass finds its way throughout China. The demand for it is so considerable that several thousands of people are constantly engaged to supply the market.

Acquaintance with foreigners has given to the Canton joiners and carpenters a great superiority above their countrymen. They therefore do not only export their furniture to other countries, but provide also their fellow citizens with a variety of elegant furniture. All small articles comprised under the name of toys, trinkets, nicknacks, &c., are here made to great perfection and the exportation is as large as that from Nuremberg in Germany. It is a common saying in China that to obtain any ingenious article you must go to Canton. There is no place like it in the Empire, where one can procure everything. It is with these manufactures that Canton pays its large exports, and thus forms a centre of industry from whence no other city has yet been able to move it.

The inhabitants, though carrying on very extensive speculation with the interior, are not famous for their maritime enterprise. The trade carried on with the East and West coast of the Province is by craft belonging to those respective districts. They bring from the sea coast raw produce amongst which salt, fish, rice and sugar are the principal. Junks from Chaou choo arrive empty and take in their cargo at Canton. These are the most numerous maritime carriers.

With Kwangse Province Canton corresponds by means of the rivers which join the Choo keang. This is the great granary and the quantities of rice which arrive from thence are very large. From hence also cassia is imported, which is in China a substitute for cinnamon and much sought for by foreigners. The Meaou tsze, a race of mountaineers who inhabit the uncultivated tracts of this province, come down the river in long narrow boats resembling the canoes of the Indians and barter for their raw produce cotton stuffs and utensils. They are a sprightly enterprising race who venture much in their frail barques in pursuit of gain.

The trade from Yunnan in metals, copper, lead, tutenague,* precious stones, betelnut, and other tropical articles (some of which are brought from Birmah), gold dust, precious stones, and other mineral productions is very considerable. But the transport is tedious and the commerce yields only small profits. Kueichoo province stands nearly in the same relation with Canton. In addition to the above mentioned articles, medical herbs, tobacco, and musk are imported from thence. But the commerce is still in its infancy, and there are few natives of that district who repair to Canton.

Of far greater importance is the commerce it carries on with Fokéén both by sea and by land. The Junks bring from thence pulse, earthenware, umbrellas, tobacco, grass cloth, and several smaller articles. From Formosa a great deal of sugar and camphor find their way to Canton, whilst the river boats import black teas. This is the most important branch of the domestic trade. More than 4,000 inhabitants of the Province (i.e., Fukien--ed.) are settled in Canton and maintain large commercial establishments. The greater part of the floating capital is in their hands and they perform extensive voyages into the interior in the capacity of brokers and agents in order to supply the market. The reexportation of foreign cotton in their bottoms is very considerable.

*Zinc (ed.)

Chekeang. The commercial relations with Chekeang are chiefly carried on with Ningpo and Hangchoo silk piece goods, raw silk, embroidery in large quantities, fans, and other fancy articles, whilst several descriptions of tea for home consumption are imported from those ports. In return they take foreign articles, especially camlets and bullion. A very high and respectable body of Ningpo merchants resides at Canton and greatly influences the market.

Keangsoo imports more than its exports amount to. Here is the great market for silks wrought and raw, nankeens, and other stuffs, ink, and various other articles of consumption. The inland trade however is the most flourishing; in the maritime trade the Fokëën and Tinghae Junks are the carriers. Of raw produce, Cotton is the only important article which finds a ready sale at Canton; it can compete in price with the Indian.

Ganhwuy. The trade from Ganhwuy is almost exclusively confined to Green teas, of which however the whole quantity prepared solely for the foreign market amounts to several millions of dollars annually. Constant demand and the late high prices of teas at Canton have induced the natives to cultivate the tea shrub to a large extent not far from the metropolis. Year after year does Canton increase its tea manufactures, though the article brings a very low price. To enhance its value they dye the leaves, after having sufficiently roasted them, with Prussian blue and gypsum, and by beautifying the color poison the teas. Though this is a fact generally known, the article meets always a ready sale and amounts since these last four years nearly to a fourth of the whole exportation of green teas. Ganhwuy merchants flock in considerable numbers to the Provincial city and reëxport a variety of foreign articles.

Central Provinces. The trade with the central Provinces is less flourishing because the reciprocal necessities are few. Keangse imports the finest porcelain, and various coarse stuffs, with drugs and other raw articles. The export trade to this province is far more considerable and the natives, a very shrewd race, repair in large numbers to Canton for the sake of trade. This country yields also some tea, of which however very little is exported to foreign countries.

Hoonan, Hoopih, and Honan provide the Canton market with musk, rhubarb, and other drugs. Szechuan sends metals and the best rhubarb, but to neither of these districts is the trade very brisk, and only few natives visit Canton.

Shanse, though very distant, keeps up a large commerce, and thus unites the distant city with the Northern part of Asia. The merchants being in possession of a great quantity of bullion repair to Canton as the most likely place where it can be laid out to great advantage, and thus carry on extensive speculation. Their chief importations are musk, rhubarb, medical herbs, and fans of every description, which they barter in Mongolia or at the frontiers of Siberia. They are the principal consumers of our woolens and buy a great many fancy articles of Europe manufacture. This is next to the Fokéén perhaps the most flourishing branch.

Shense and Kansuh carry on a similar trade with Canton. There are several rich bankers from the former province at the metropolis who influence the market considerably. The goods are transported by water to the Yellow River and thence forwarded by the large roads. The trade in precious stones and agates engages many individuals.

Shantung receives by the inland navigation Canton manufactures to a very small amount--sugar and other Indian produce with a variety of silks and cotton stuffs, but the trade is on the whole very trifling. The return cargoes consist of winter fruit, hempen stuffs, and cabbage.

Chihle and especially the capital carries on a very extensive speculation with Canton, from whence it obtains every article of European art and manufacture, and a thousand trifles which may be numbered amongst the luxuries of life. There is a constant influx of Canton goods, and even Mandarins who proceed from that city to the Capital do not scruple to become merchants on a very large scale. Several of the most powerful dignitaries of the Empire keep their agents in constant employ to forward to them whatever pleases their fancy. The returns consist principally of bullion, carpets, felt, and dates.

The foreign trade carried on in Canton bottoms in the southern islands also is very considerable, though not at all to be compared to the home commerce. In all the harbours where they touch, a number of Chinese Colonists are living who are the principal consumers of the imports. Incense sticks, tinned paper, of which there are very large manufactures in Canton, China ware, lackered articles, cotton, and silk stuffs, with every other article of Chinese luxury makes up the cargo. These vessels however are generally owned by Chaou choo men, and are seldom freighted by single individuals, and even the sailors have a share in the cargo. The craft vary from 150-500 tons, and they not merely carry goods but often several hundreds of emigrants. This trade was 12-20 years ago very flourishing, but since the Dutch and Spaniards have laid high duties upon the goods, and since lately many Junks have been wrecked, native capitalists prefer Portuguese ships for embarking their property, so that the commerce may be said to be on a decline.

Trade with Tonkin. Of the trade which is carried on between Canton and Tonkin by land we know very little; but there exists a considerable traffic in raw silk, hides, dyestuffs, and tropical articles. Both Governments are equally averse to foreign intercourse, but the natives with their customary adroitness elude the prohibitions and engage largely in smuggling. Tonkin for many years has been entirely shut against foreign trade; the only remaining commercial relation, with China, has thereby gained in extensiveness. Chinese emigrants have settled wherever the Government would permit them, and not satisfied with the inland trade, Canton merchants fit out annually four or five Junks for Cachao, where they import earthenware, tin paper, incense, coarse lackered ware, umbrellas etc. and fetch the above mentioned articles. The natives are very poor, bullion is very scarce, and the greater part of the trade is mere barter.

Trade with Cochin China. Canton sends also from 8-12 large Junks, the property of Tinghae citizens, to Saegon, and other harbours of Cochinchina. The imports are nearly the same as the above, but the exports are principally betel nut and sugar, of which little is brought to Canton, but by far the greater part sold at Shanghai and Teentsin.

Of far greater importance is the commerce with Siam, which employs on an average 20-30 Junks, the major part of which is the property of Siamese or Chinese who are living in that country, but they are manned with natives from the Province. All of them take in their cargoes at Canton or Macao, consisting of various manufactures, fruits, and delicacies, with incense sticks and a variety of other trifles. They bring in return sugar, ivory, Sapan wood, gamboge, and a great variety of other articles, lately also rice. Most of these goods go to the Northern Provinces and the Junks return with peas, flour, mutton, and other kinds of provisions to Canton. These speculations turn out so advantageously that there are few engaged in them who do not amass considerable capital. They are in fact viewed as the most profitable branches of the whole maritime commerce. The vessels proceed to two ports only, viz., Cantibun and Bankok; the latter is the capital of the country.

There are from two to four large Junks of 500-700 tons burthen annually sent to the island of Borneo, which visit the gold mines near Pantianak, Banjermassing, and Sambas, where a Chinese republic numbering more than 60,000 individuals has been established since many years. The cargoes are richer than those to other parts of the Archipelago, whilst the gold remitted annually to China is said to amount to no less than 12 peculs. Buttons, ebony, and tin are the staple articles which are brought from thence. But the adventures to this part of the world are precarious, and many Junks have lately been lost in their attempt to reach the island.

Four or six large vessels go to Singapore. The cargoes are nearly the same as above, though they also take goods for the Furopean market. Here they receive straits produce, Europe manufactures, and the poisonous drug opium. The exports are far more durable than the imports, because the emigrants who wish to return home invest their hard earnings in various ways. These Junks bring a great many colonists whom necessity drives from their country. They are extremely poor and many become prey to disease and a premature death before they have earned one single pice. Yet are these emigrants still on the increase, and every season pours out new thousands for the cultivation of the islands of the Archipelago.

Several of those Junks go also to Sumarung and Rhio, and having there unloaded their goods, take in the produce of the country with a number of passengers, then retrace their steps to Singapore, where they fill up their cargoes.

This trade, though the Chinese have to enter in competition with Europeans, is nevertheless very flourishing, and extends more and more. There are several articles much in demand in China of which our merchants have never become competent judges, and therefore unable to traffic in them. Such are bird's nests, bichedemar (bêche de mer), agar agar, &c, which Chinamen alone understand to buy, to suit the market of their country. Pepper is a spice very much in demand in the northern Provinces, and Keangnan consumes immense quantities. The trade carried on in British manufactures had hitherto been very small. To account for this we ought to remember that the greater part of the capital is invested in poisonous opium, which yields far more profitable returns, and finds always a ready sale. Most of our woollens are bought by private individuals and are often sold at 30 per cent clear profit. Some years ago the Junks attempted to supply Singapore with teas for home consumption. These came from Ankoi and having proved to be of the worst description, this branch of commerce soon ceased of its own accord.

In former times from 4-5 Junks went annually to Java. They were of the largest description, and navigated by Portuguese pilots. The profits were so large that notwithstanding the wreck of so many vessels the voyages still prove lucrative. Since however the Dutch have laid heavy duties upon Chinese merchandise and shackled the trade in various other ways, it is now confined to one or two vessels.

The commerce to Banka and Palembang is still carried on unabated, the principal articles which the Chinese export from thence are tin and rattans, but the adventures to these ports are not regular.

This is the whole foreign commerce of Canton carried on in native bottoms, which employs (not including the small Haenan craft) from 40-50 large vessels of 200-600 tons burthen, requires at the highest calculation a capital of 5 millions of dollars, and does not amount to a sixth part of the maritime trade of this city to the other Provinces. It is therefore looked upon by the Chinese Government with studied contempt, and though connived in, by no means legalized. It is true that Keen lung* at the commencement of his reign issued an edict by which

*Ch'ien Lung (ed.)

he allowed his subjects to visit foreign parts, especially in order to buy rice, but notwithstanding this wide stretch of imperial favor, a merchant returning from India may be brought before a court of justice and sentenced to death as a traitor to his country for having had commercial intercourse with foreigners. Though such instances of arbitrary rule are at present less frequent, no man wishes to embark a very large capital in these adventures, and by far the greater part of the business is carried on by mere pedlars who charter a small part of the Junks in which they proceed as passengers. In times of yore Chinese Junks of an immense size passed the Straits of Malacca and proceeded to Hindostan and the Persian Gulf, but at present no vessel that comes direct from China ventures as far as Pulo Penang. The greater cheapness and dispatch of European sailing vessels have made it impracticable to the Chinese to cope with Western nations. Soon they will be brought to the dire dilemma of either improving with other nations or being entirely cut off from navigating the Archipelago.

Foreign Commerce. About the commerce carried on by the various nations of Europe and America so much has lately been written that we shall not enter into details and only dwell upon such subjects which come under the immediate attention of our Government. Its progressive rate may be seen from the statements published annually by the chamber of commerce. It has firmly taken root, insinuated itself into all the native channels of trade, and is so interwoven with national prosperity that to cut it off would be aiming a deathblow at the public welfare. China in the fullest sense of the word has come into the commercial wheel; attempt to stop it and it will either crush the daring hand of him who endeavours to do so, or reduce every branch of industry to a state of stagnation.

We shall not dwell upon the many thousands of natives who maintain themselves entirely by cultivating, transporting, and selling teas and silks, nor point out the gains which Canton itself directly derives from it. But there is a class of men who are here as well as anywhere else the most influential, and find it their greatest interest to uphold foreign commerce. We allude to the capitalists who flock hither from all parts of the Empire, and circulate their money to the highest advantages in these various branches of commerce. It is by their means that the most binding connections are kept up with the principal cities of China. A sudden stoppage of the trade renders their capital either useless or puts it into Jeopardy, and it is on this account that they never would acquiesce in such a measure, but with magic influence of money set it again in motion. Many officers of high rank and wealth embark their treasures in this profitable trade, and are thus deeply interested in its prosperity. Waiving even the considerable sums which it adds to the revenues, another great advantage arises from it by giving to the country a constant supply of circulating medium. After all that has been written about the great exportation of bullion from China during the last two years at an average of 6-8 millions per annum, it has not yet been proved that much sycee silver has been exported. The simple fact however that large quantities of dollars are current in every commercial town is the best and most conclusive evidence that the total importation exceeds by far the exportation. Let the source however be stopped and the greatest misery would very soon be felt. Not only would the common people be forced to substitute cumbersome cash for silver, but even the payments made to Government must be in this unwieldy article. Such things have taken place and are still bitterly complained of by the Emperor himself. The pecuniary embarrassment would doubtless be extreme under such circumstances, and again force the trade open.

We have thus merely referred to the high orders whose very interests guarantee the continuance of the foreign trade. Perhaps the mass of the people, though counted as nothing by the rulers of China, exert a decided influence upon its preservation. When during the latter end of 1837 the trade was reduced to its lowest ebb on account of the failures in England and America and some regulations of the Governor, the merchants uttered the bitterest complaints against the latter and openly accused him at the throne of malversation. So powerful was the stream which set in against this grandee that he was obliged to remodel all his measures and send a paper in his Justification to the Emperor. Suppose that a total stoppage could take place for any length of time, what might have been the case in such a populous city as Canton? Even if the Governor had received strict orders from the court, he would not have put the patience of the ruled to such a severe test, and under some pretence or other either have deferred the execution or carry the orders into effect for a very limited space of time. It is our firm conviction that this commerce is no longer entirely in the grasp of Government, and that the mandarins on account of its magnitude and paramount influence are unable to manage it as they please. The basis upon which it stands, strong self-interest, is broad and firm as a rock. So long as the present order of things exists nothing will shake it, whatever the temporary measures to impede its progress. We have nothing to fear on that score, and the only danger which might arise would be from a revolution by which the present dynasty might be expelled. Such an event in a despotic country like China, which is ruled by a handful of foreigners, is not at all improbable. The monarch is verging towards sixty, the presumptive heir to the throne a child, and the mass of the people are much oppressed, whilst the influential officers are at variance. Still many years may elapse before such a direful calamity may happen; and even in that case the foreign influence judiciously exerted might do much to avert the ruin of the trade.

Four years have now elapsed since the opening of the trade to free merchants. Many predictions made by the opponents to this measure have literally been verified, whilst others have proved merely imaginary. The natives themselves expressed neither great hopes nor fears, but viewed this measure with apathy. The Tea Men, however, very soon perceived that the great competition in the market greatly enhanced the price of their goods. They made in a short time large profits and began to speculate wildly. Several Hong merchants laid hold of this favourable moment, and instead of confining themselves to sales at Canton, they sent large cargoes of teas to Europe. The funds for these adventures would on account of the Company's finance committee be easily raised, and they foolishly presumed that since the teas fetched such a high price above the prime cost on the spot, there ought to be a proportionable large price in the countries where they were consumed. But they were very soon undeceived, and most of their speculations proved an utter failure, entailing not seldom a loss of 30 per cent. Yet the tea and silk men were more successful; every season raised in them new hopes until the dismal Autumn of 1837. All their expectations were then utterly dashed to the ground. Many were irrevocably ruined and a deep gloom overspread the whole fraternity. From this panic they are now gradually recovering, but at the same time the general wish of all concerned is that the golden times of the company might return. Then there were no such fluctuations, the profits were always sure, and the trade went on as regular as clock work.

Such is the public opinion of the Cantonese, and this will remain the same until that unequal and injurious struggle between free trade and the Hong monopoly has ended in the total overthrow of the latter.

The Hong Merchants. The business of the Hong merchants has lately been brought before the public, not as something new but as an irremediable evil of long standing. Debts were formerly run up as well as during the last four years, but never to such a large amount. The whole system of the Hongs has proved to be entirely ruinous in its very principles, and more than a hundred years' experience have shewn that immense failures are the order of the day and in fact unavoidable.

At the very opening of a Hong, considerable sums must be paid into the hand of the Mandarins, which swallows up a great part of the capital of the beginner or plunges him from the very commencement into debt. He must moreover keep up an establishment, which including all expenses will cost him annually from 50-60,000 dollars, and to realise this sum, great profits and a very flourishing business become necessary. If he however retains some money of his own, he may keep himself from pecuniary embarrassments, and with prudent management earn the sums requisite for continuing his firm. Out of five individuals, however, there is not one who has this good fortune. To carry on business they are therefore obliged to take up money at 12-20 per cent of interests, and thus involve themselves in insurmountable difficulties. Fully aware, however, that within less than ten years their affairs will be utterly hopeless, they secret as much of the disposable money as they can and provide for their children and relations either by buying offices or settling them respectably in life, that they may have friends in time of need. Upon this general course are very few exceptions. The three individuals who at present have a considerable capital at their command have realised it by engaging in very lucrative speculations with foreign merchants as their partners and abstaining almost entirely from trading in the customary way. This is the business of the poorer Hongs, which are obliged to buy dear and sell cheap merely to keep themselves from sinking, and to add debt upon debt as long as they can obtain any credit or to act merely as brokers.

The Government hastens failures. The Government doubtless participates in the guilt of increasing the evils of this vicious system. Besides the constant drain upon the treasury of the Hong merchants, the very fact that they are the toys of the Mandarins destroys their credit amongst their countrymen. It moreover recognizes no debts contracted with natives, often designates them with the opprobrious epithet of traitors, and repeatedly has laid hands on very respectable merchants, who by being made an object of its vengeance were either totally ruined or could never regain their credit. The system however in itself is radically wrong, and encloses a gnawing and destructive cankerworm in its very core. So long as the monopoly of the Company lasted, many falling Hongs could be upheld by the monied interest of such a powerful body, but this prop being taken away, the whole structure must ere long fall to pieces with a tremendous crash. One untoward circumstance, be it the death of the senior HowKwa, an extraordinary exaction of Government, or the seizure of the richer members, will produce this crisis.

Hong merchants debts. The late failure of Hing tae's Hong, the largest which has ever yet happened, has brought to light the most extraordinary condition of this company. Their confessions were not extorted by foreigners, but freely published in order to induce creditors to defer their claims. There is one circumstance which must strike one very forcibly, and this is that within the last four years the trade has been more flourishing than at any preceding period, and that during this time the debts incurred have been most enormous. The conclusion which some natives have drawn from it is that the more flourishing the trade the greater the liability of the Hongs to involve themselves. During this time they had to clear off no old scores, which has almost always been the case, the money they received for the Consoo charges amounted to more than a million, the teas were sold at a high price, and yet notwithstanding all their advantages, nearly 5 millions of dollars were run up in debts, and most Hongs got into commercial difficulties from which they will never be able to extricate themselves.

Upon this the Hong merchants have resolved to clear off the debts within ten years, forgetting at the same time that most of the fraternity have not a single farthing for liquidating them, and that within the prescribed time, large failures must again take place, and this the sooner since the respective houses have never been in a more deplorable condition. It can not be expected that under such circumstances men of large property will join the company, or that the Government's proclamations will raise the credit of the Hongs. An assessment upon foreign trade much more heavy than it was ever before must therefore take place, and all the foreign merchants in a body bear the burden of paying the debts of the Hongs. Whatever at present is put upon foreign commerce will never be taken off again how much soever the circumstances may change, and the legal trade will thus be more and more burthened. According to the last regulations, the Consoo charge upon some articles was no less than 10 per cent ad valorem. A moment's consideration will show that the taxation thus entailed upon the foreign trade and the difficulties accruing from the bankrupt condition of the Hongs are most injurious to British interests. The commerce may drag its existence, even the present large debts may be paid by the foreign merchants through the Hong merchants to themselves, but its tendency will always be ruinous, and give rise to a series of practical difficulties which will end in a most violent collision.

The advantages of the Hongs ought at the same time not to be overlooked. In a country where no foreigner has access to a court of Justice, where cunning and craft are carried to a very great length, and where the foreign merchant is confined to a single suburb, it is easily to be understood that he would lose all hold upon the native dealer if Government did not guarantee the payments of the sums due to him from its own merchants. This is too well understood by all parties to require any explanation in order to show the necessity of the Hongs. The Government moreover wants men upon whom it may throw all the responsibility, whom it may punish for any misdemeanor, and through whom it may fine the foreign merchants, and receive the legal duties. All these purposes have been answered by the establishment of the Hongs, and whilst these merchants are ministers of foreign affairs and the police of the factories, they are scapegoats of Government in every respect. Yet whatever may be their personal sufferings, which have been now and then cruel and severe in the extreme, the pecuniary sacrifices they have to make are reimbursed by foreigners. Whether voluntary contributions, presents, or extortions, the foreign trade pays for all, and it is their task only to devise means for raising the funds.

Viewed in this light, the Mandarins will be very loath to abolish such a convenient company. Let the commercial difficulties be ever so great, so long as the duties are regularly paid and the exactions readily discharged, old custom will be pleaded in favor of the continuance of the Hongs; and as the lives of the merchants would be in jeopardy if they regulated this service, they are not likely to prove refractory.

The faltering state of the Hongs. On the other hand, this monopoly has become so insufferable and so frequently been supplanted by the industry and enterprise of outside merchants that even a bigoted Government will theoretically allow that it is no longer tenable. Though this avowal has never been officially made, yet are the difficulties into which the rulers themselves are involved so multifarious that they are fully aware of the rottenness of the system.

It has repeatedly been asked what is then to be substituted for the Hongs? and this important question has never yet satisfactorily been answered. Every step to be taken must be preceeded by a perfect understanding between the two Governments which are most interested in setting this knotty point. As this desirable object, however, has not yet been realised, it would only be premature to agitate a question which we are at present utterly unable to solve.

In reconsidering, however, the chances of carrying on a trade under such great disadvantages, we ought never to forget that the interests being divided, each individual endeavors, by hook and crook, to manage his own business. When however large cargoes are to be disposed of, and credit must necessarily be given on account of the inability of the buyers to pay in ready money, the risk to which a foreign merchant is exposed will always be very considerable. To engage with outside merchants in any dealings of importance may entail a total loss of property without the most distant hope of recovering it. There are other evils as annoying for the foreigners as for the natives which attend any legal transactions with the Hongs. Still this vigorous trade may successfully wrestle with these obstacles, though at the same time illegalities will increase in the same ratio as the exactions become more heavy.

Prospects of the foreign trade in general. The prospects of the foreign trade are very fair. It extends its sway wider and wider, and it may reasonably be expected that the Government will be obliged to legalize the commerce to the Northern Ports. It would be in vain to fix upon the period when this event may take place, since various circumstances may either retard or accelerate it. But the flood gates have been opened and to restrain the strong current would be lost labour. The edicts against sailing in the inner waters near the shores of the Celestial Empire have been entirely disregarded, and the constant presence of foreign vessels has accustomed the Mandarins to take the same course as their fellow officers at Canton. But it is deeply to be regretted that opium should be the staple article and smuggling precede the legal commerce. Of this inconvenience, however, the local authorities are not aware, for the legal traffic, though filling the chests of the Emperor, brings nothing into their pockets, and they are therefore most determinately opposed to any legalization. This is perhaps one of the greatest obstacles to improvements and to placing the commerce on a fair footing. Whatever measures lessen the chances of bribes, how exalted soever and beneficial for the interests of the country at large, will be most strongly counteracted by the men in power.

A British resident at the Captial. The British commercial interest, the contiguity of the Chinese territory to our Indian frontiers, and even the political relations with Russia render the residence of a chargé d'affaires at Peking no longer a matter of choice but of necessity. We bring this subject forward because it is our humble opinion that a resident ought first to have taken up his abode at Peking before the local government at Canton will be induced to treat without interference of the Hong merchants with a British credited officer. The difficulties, however, of achieving this object have hitherto appeared so formidable as to render the subject almost impracticable, and unless we ourselves adopt a different course it is not likely that it can be ever gained. The Chinese cannot be treated according to our diplomatical code; they ought to be approached as Asiatics, and as a people distinct from the whole human race, in fact as Chinamen. Our guides in opening this intercourse are our previous failures arrayed as warning beacons along our road to the Capital. All similar enterprises are sure to miscarry, because the Chinese will fail us with the same weapons as they did before. Canton ought never under any consideration to be made the scene of negotiations, and a steady unwearying course once adopted should be persevered in to the last. We can moreover not expect that the Chinese will come down to us; for this they are too proud, too ignorant, and too much afraid, but we must go to them.

Voyages along the Coast. As a preliminary measure we should suggest a friendly visit to all the principal Emporiums of the Coast in one of the Hong merchants' ships. The writer has again and again witnessed how easy the access is in those unfrequented parts to the highest dignitaries. Some have sat down for hours to listen to the conversation of foreigners, and even to make notes of their observations. Nor have those discussions been entirely in vain, and besides giving a deep insight into the Chinese character in general, and especially of the Government, friendly feelings have been generated on both sides. It is now six years since the Amherst first visited the shores of this country and Mr. Lindsay the supercargo is still remembered with a cordiality of which we might think a Mandarin quite incapable. How deep and lasting was the impression made by this voyage the writer himself can testify, since at a second trip some very influential civilians inquired whether any proposals for coming to a better understanding had been drawn up. If such an expedition was accompanied by intelligent men, endowed with firmness and great patience, the result would doubtless prove very favourable, and accustom the Mandarins to have intercourse with British functionaries. It might then not be difficult to adopt suitable measures, after due and ample investigation in accordance with the results of these expeditions, and to take further steps for accomplishing our purpose. As the Russians have gained their point, we ought not despair of success, but to advance at a steady pace towards the desired end whilst maintaining an unvarying conduct calculated to produce effect. The unfavorable impressions which almost seem to preclude the possibility of coming to a definite arrangement have been received at Canton, where so many things coöperate to render every attempt nugatory. Hence, nothing more should be undertaken in that quarter, and the whole matter put beyond the reach of the local authorities of that city.

It is well worth it to extend our trade with this Empire and to adopt a steady course which will lead to this desirable end. The objections against this proposal have been various, but they were not founded upon a knowledge of localities, and deducted from the general belief that the Chinese themselves were averse to foreign trade. The Government determined upon never granting this boon, because the Western powers made the same restrictions. Such arguments have paralysed all efforts and even the question itself is no longer agitated, yet the subject ought to be fairly discussed and no inferences be drawn before suitable attempts have been made to ascertain the real state of the case. If it can be proven that the sale of manufactures would not increase, and the articles of British consumption not be cheapened by having access to other ports, it would not be worth the trouble to reason upon the matter. But both those surmises militate against experience and do not deserve a reputation. The Chinese merchants are eager to have dealings with foreigners, and would hail the arrival of ships in their harbours; this has sufficiently been proved in the recent voyages. If we permit Chinese vessels to come to all our Emporiums, and they avail themselves of this privilege as far as the Junks are able to go, it would not be so very wrong to ask the same prerogative to have liberty for trading to three or four emporiums. The Government however is most obstinate against such an innovation, and to overcome its prejudices ought to be our first care. As the present state of affairs loudly calls for a better understanding with the court of Peking, and measures must sooner or later be taken to realise this desideratum, no pains should be spared for bringing some other harbours open to British enterprise. The objections made by the Mandarins are so shallow that they can easily be refuted; and when this is once satisfactorily done we shall have approached nearer the goal of our wishes.

R. M. MARTIN

MINUTE ON THE BRITISH POSITION AND PROSPECTS IN CHINA

Hong Kong, 19 April 1845

It is of great importance to examine our present novel and somewhat anomalous position in China; to ascertain what are our prospects in various points of view; and to trace the line of policy which national interests in combinations with national responsibility would indicate as the most advisable course to be pursued with reference to the mutual benefit of Great Britain and the vast Chinese Empire.

For two centuries Britain carried on a restricted commercial intercourse with one port of China through the medium of a well-organised mercantile Company; China was politically isolated from all other nations, and our sole object was to maintain in peace a profitable trade subject to the control and not unfrequent interruption of a haughty, jealous, and exclusive Government.

Our open, extensive, and unceasing prosecution of a traffic in a prohibited and pernicious drug was necessarily followed by violent acts on the part of a proud and determined viceroy, whose power was unequal to his will and who resorted to the only means at his command for the forcible suppression of what was deemed by his Sovereign a grievous evil fraught with great injury and suffering to the people and country at large. The result was soon manifested: England, much against her inclination, was compelled to declare war against the Government of China; the Chinese, whether by sea or by land, were everywhere easily discomfitted; the momentary fight was soon converted into an indiscriminate slaughter; fire suicide completed the dreadful havoc; the conquered cities became in several instances scenes of plunder, desolation, and anarchy; commerce was interrupted, and inland communication cut off, and finally the Chinese Government was compelled to sue for peace, and to pay the whole of the <u>then</u> estimated expenses of the war, to permit resort to four other ports as well as to Canton, to reduce their customs duties and Port Charges, and to cede an island to Great Britain on which a Colonial Establishment could be maintained for the protection of British commerce, for the development of civilization of the frontiers of the Chinese Empire, and which would not only serve as a guarantee for the future, but which would aid in preserving peace between the two countries.

English interests are now therefore irrevocably interwoven with those of China; we hold the largest stake at issue as regards her peaceful prosperity and national independence, and whatever strengthens our power, extends our commerce, and permanently enlarges our influence, is equally beneficial to China and to England. Other nations have since come forward to claim a participation in the concessions obtained by

Britain. Treaties have been arranged with the United States and France, and China for the first time has entered into the social compact which Kingdoms as well as individuals find necessary for their protection, and which, rightly understood, is indispensable to their tranquility and to their improvement.

The far-seeing Politician must therefore admit that sooner or later China (whose inhabitants it is estimated number one third of the human race) will exercise an important influence on the Affairs of Europe. How this influence will be primarily manifested, whether through India or through Russia, or by reason of European nations contending for a dominant Power in this vast Empire, it seems impossible to predicate, but this much is evident, that no nation is so deeply interested in the "Chinese Question" as Britain; that this interest must daily increase on political, maritime, and mercantile considerations, and that a solemn responsibility has devolved on Great Britain in relation to China which cannot be neglected without involving serious and perhaps irretrievable calamities.

There probably never was a period in our history when greater civil, intellectual, and moral efforts were necessary for the preservation of our position among competitive surrounding nations. And it is advantageous for us that these efforts should be made: Britain cannot remain stationary; she must either retrogade or advance. Happily her advancement rightly directed is beneficial to all mankind, by enabling her to maintain the peace of the world, to promote civilization, to reclaim the savage to till the waste regions of the earth, and to fulfill her high vocation by a widespread dissemination of the inestimable blessings of Christianity.

A Republic of nations is as Utopian in the existing selfishness of mankind as a Republic of individuals, and the maintenance of one Kingdom sufficiently supreme to protect weaker Kingdoms, to preserve order, to uphold the reign of law, and to inculcate by precept and by example the duties which the possession of Great Power involves is essential to the steady and triumphant progress of true civilization. No nation is so well adapted for this supreme control as Britain by reason of her insularity, her tolerant religion, her free Institutions, her distant and varied Colonial Possessions, her non-alliance with continental intrigues, her obvious policy to maintain peace, and her maritime superiority which leaves no desire for continental aggrandizement in Europe.

Whether these views be acquiesced in or not by other nations, it is equally the duty of Britain to maintain this supreme control. To do so she must take fair advantage of every circumstance which may contribute to its maintenance by extending her commerce and by establishing her influence in new and distant regions.

To this course of Policy Britain is also urged by domestic considerations, namely by the increasing pressure of population of the means of subsistence, by inventions of machinery which daily diminishes the demand for human labour, by a constant accumulation of capital which requires a profitable investment, and by a general system of education which while elevating the whole of the nation renders mere animal toil irksome, and demands a higher grade of occupation at home or abroad for the intelligent masses of society.

The premises thus set forth being granted, a statesman will survey the field on which he has to operate. He beholds in Europe and in America a career of successful competition with Britain in the manufactures and produce which the British Empire can abundantly furnish; he sees little or no reciprocity of free trade, but on the contrary the adoption of a more exclusive system; he ascertains that foreign manufactures now not unfrequently displace our goods in distant markets, of which we had heretofore a complete monopoly. To the British Colonial Possessions and to new unexplored regions must England look for the increase of her commerce. The East and the West Indies, the Canadas, Australia, and Africa afford valuable and permanent markets within our control, but excepting India their expansion is of slow growth, and inadequate to meet increasing exigencies. The opening therefore of the vast and populous territories on the borders of the northern Pacific is a matter of vital consequence to Britain.

Have we availed ourselves of the advantages which this opening affords? Have we not by a mistaken Policy and by a non-appreciation of the true interests of England almost shut the door against ourselves which we had been so long anxious to open and virtually voluntarily excluded the British nation from a country where it is palpably our interest to have a decided permanent influence, and where by our science, intercourse, and commerce we may exert a beneficial effect on many millions of mankind?

The solution of these questions is deserving of early and serious investigation.

At the close of a desolating and expensive war in August 1842, in a position to dictate our own terms and when all negotiation was unnecessary and set aside by the Chinese authorities themselves* the British Plenipotentiary adopted the printed draft of a treaty framed in Downing Street and sent out to Capt. Elliot for his guidance at Canton. This treaty was prepared at a time when we were ignorant on various points connected with China and great allowance must be made for its Framers. Without therefore that Diplomatic tact or foresight which an acquaintance with

* It is perfectly well known that when Lt. Colonel Malcolm was sent on shore at Nankin with the terms on which peace would be granted, the Imperial Commissioner was surprised that so little was asked and enquired "Is that all?", which being answered affirmatively, he immediately replied, "All shall be granted."

European Policy, and British domestic as well as foreign interest would have conveyed, and without reference to the new position in which we were at Nankin, and to the greater knowledge we had obtained of the people and country in the North of China, we imposed only the terms sketched in the draft treaty and filled up the blank after the word "islands" in the Draft with Hong Kong and excluded Chusan, the only valuable island on the Coast of China adapted for the great purposes which England ought to have had in view.

A primary condition of the Treaty was the payment by the Chinese Government of a sum of money then deemed adequate to the expenses of the war. It is now, however, confidently stated by commissariat officers that the sum of money thus obtained will not cover the mere pecuniary expenditure incurred by Great Britain after paying for the alleged destruction of Opium, for the Hong debts and the prize money to the Army and the Navy, irrespective of the loss of troops by sickness, each of whom costs the state £100. But it having been agreed that the so-called indemnity should be paid by the Chinese Government in half-yearly installments spreading over a period of three years and a half, the maintenance of a naval and military force in China at a cost of nearly £500,000 annually was deemed necessary. It can scarcely therefore be contended that the "Indemnity Money" was to the extent alleged of such great advantage, and that the British Exchequer has not suffered considerable diminution by the war with China.

The next great advantage which it was supposed we had gained was the establishment of four New Ports for British trade as named in the printed draft treaty sent from Downing Street. Our obvious and natural Policy was to cause every port in China to be opened to us and to have obtained perfect freedom of ingress and egress to and from any city, town, or place in China, with secure guarantees for life and property and the peaceable and unrestricted prosecution of Commerce. This would have enabled our Traders to seek out the best spots for mercantile settlement, and time and circumstances would thus have indicated and proven the most suitable market for extensive traffic. But if it had even been resolved to restrict the maritime trade to a few ports in order that the Chinese Customs' Revenue might have been more readily collected, it was our duty to have selected very different Ports from those which through want of information were selected in Downing Street, and which at any rate ought to have been preceded by a Commission of enquiry as to their eligibility for European traffic.

Nankin, great central mart of the Chinese Empire, Yangchoofoo on the North Bank and Chinkiangfoo on the South Bank of the great Yangtze kiang, were neglected, together with the numerous Cities and Towns bordering on this vast artery which it is said extends through the richest regions of China for 1800 miles, Chapoo, the port of Hangchow, as large as Canton, and the seat of trade with Japan, Haouchoofoo on the Northern and Tingchoofoo on the Southern part of the Shantung promontory, Tientzin on the Peiho, the Port of Peking, and Kichu and Kinchu on the Northern Part of the gulf of Pechelee in 40° to 41° North, rich in agricultural productions and good stations for trade with Tartary.

Those and other important places were lost sight of in our hasty, restricted, and ill-arranged proceedings. We allowed our attention to be diverted from the rich and populous regions at the Northern and Central part of the Empire to the comparatively barren and valueless coast at its Southern extremity. Even at the Ports chosen for our Maritime trade we took no precautions to secure freedom of access and to right of trade* and residence at and in the Cities to which these Ports were attached and which it is understood the present Plenipotentiary of Her Majesty is now strenuously and laudably endeavouring to accomplish. This is manifest as regards Canton, where we are still confined to a few feet of occupation of the left bank of the river outside the suburbs of the city, daily insulted and with life and property exposed to continual risk. We are prohibited sending a boat for pleasure or for traffic to Futchan, a thriving manufacturing town about 20 miles above Canton, or to Chankingfoo and Shaou chao foo on the same river, as it is said nearly as large and wealthy as Canton. The same may be said of the city of Chang-chow-foo a few miles above Amoy, of which city Amoy is but the Outlet, so also of Suchoo of which Shanghai is only the Port. It would be as absurd of the French or any other nation to say they were admitted to freedom of trade with England if we permitted them an anchorage at Gravesend on the bank of the Thames and a few feet of ground for a residence at Rotherhithe or Wapping for London, at Pill for Bristol, at Birkenhead for Liverpool, at Cobh for Cork, or at Greenock for Glasgow. Of the four selected ports, three, Amoy, Foochoo, and Ningpo, have scarcely any foreign trade, and do not appear likely ever to have any of great importance, unless we had perfect freedom of internal intercourse and could also trade between the above named ports and Formosa, an island rich in tropical productions and with which an extensive traffic is carried on from the mainland in sugar, oil, camphor, &c. The Province of Fokien, like that of Canton, is very barren and comparatively poor. Our object should have been the formation of establishments at the far richer and more civilized cities bordering on the Delta of the Yangtze Kiang and other rivers to the Northward. So long as we are confined to the coast and denied access to the great rivers and cities in the interior, our trade will be stunted or subject to con-

*Even a bazaar for the supply of provisions to the large fleet of English ships usually lying at Whampoa has been prohibited by the Authorities.

siderable fluctuations, but when enabled to traverse the great rivers and arteries of this vast Empire, to navigate with steam to the central and civilized cities which cover the land, we may look forward to an augmenting and steady trade, and to an intimate friendly intercourse fraught with mutual advantages to China and to Britain.

In obtaining a reduction of the duties on commerce and a diminution of unequal Port charges we omitted to procure an exemption from goods paying duties a second time when found unsaleable at one port and transshipped to another; and also that vessels not "breaking bulk", i. e., not discharging any part of their cargo, should be exempt from Port dues. These rights have since been gained by the Americans and we shall derive similar advantages, but we should have obtained the establishment of "Bonded Warehouses", and as the Port dues are still heavy, we should have required that a Light House be placed at the Entrance of each Port for their safe navigation. As regards Lights, Buoys, and moorings, no expense whatever has been incurred by the Chinese Government. The tonnage duties on a ship anchoring at Whampoa about 12 miles from Canton is about 3/ pr ton; at the Port of Liverpool the anchorage duty is only <u>ninepence.</u> There is a heavy outlay incurred by ships being kept at Whampoa instead of proceeding direct to Canton, which is equally as accessible as the Port of Calcutta, in the cost of loading and unloading, in the tedious transfer of Goods to and from Canton, and in the charges for provisions at Whampoa being enhanced by the "Comprador system" from which Mandarins derive a considerable revenue.

Further, the levy of one mace (about 5/ per ton on British coasting and legally licensed vessels <u>every time</u> they enter the port of Canton) is a heavy tax on craft which pass from Hong Kong to Canton three or four times in the month. Until the supplementary treaty of 8th October 1843, the number of schooners, sloops and Lorchas plying between Canton and the places in the vicinity was upwards of seventy; by Article XVII of the supplementary treaty all these vessels up to 150 tons burthen are subjected to a Port duty at Canton of one mace per ton "<u>every time</u> they enter the port". None of these vessels are allowed to be rated (however small) at less than <u>seventy-five</u> tons; thus the mere tonnage duty on the smallest cargo boat would, at 5d/ton, and entering the port of Canton four times every month, be equivalent to a tax of £15 a year.

It is not surprising that there are but a few Lorchas plying between Hong Kong and Canton. Moreover, these small vessels are obliged "on passing the Bogue forts in the Canton river to report like a large inward bound vessel" "to report herself at the Custom house at Whampoa; on arriving at Canton her sailing letter (register) to be deposited with the British Consul who will obtain permission from the Superintendent of Customs to discharge and load". "Whether with full or half lading even to an hundred weight of cargo." The smallest boat must pay at the rate of 5d (one mace) per ton on 75 tons. This enactment and clauses 13 and 14 of the supplemental treaty restricting all communication between Hong Kong and the coast of China to the five ports; requiring that "whenever the Chinese wish to take goods to Hong Kong for sale they must first pay the duties according to the new regulations at the five ports and obtain permits from the respective Custom houses"; that "the Chinese must ask a passport for coming and going, and the duties are to be paid on the day the goods are imported" that "the Chinese having purchased goods must ship them and bring them home in Chinese vessels, which must request passports at Hong Kong, and exhibit the same to the Chinese officers on each arrival and departure to be examined and counter signed" that "the Customs houses at the five ports shall monthly make out a report of passes granted with the names of the vessels and merchants and the description and amount of goods to be sent to the Comm^{r} of Customs at Canton in a prescribed form month by month. This enactment and these clauses have, it is now fully acknowledged, struck a severe blow at the coasting trade; the duty and restrictions on the Lorchas and small craft rendering them too expensive and the regulations on the Chinese vessels effectually prohibiting them from ever daring to ask for passes to trade with Hong Kong.

The supplemental treaty appears to have been most craftily designed for destroying any prospective benefit that Hong Kong might possibly have derived from the usual energy and enterprise of British merchants. Indeed it is asserted by Mr. Gutzlaff that while the treaty was negotiating a proposition was seriously entertained of stationing a Chinese Mandarin at Hong Kong for collection of the duties to be levied here on behalf of the Chinese Government.

An examination of the Chinese Tariff will show that the Export duties levied by the Chinese Government are very heavy. On tea, the export duty ranges from 12 to 20 percent; on camphor, 12 to 15 percent; on cassia, 12 percent, and so on in various proportions throughout the Tariff. It is also confidently stated that the inland Transit duties on British manufactures are still maintained at a high rate, and that our manufactures are thus effectually excluded from extended consumption in the interior of the country. The effect of transit duties on impeding the sale of goods has been manifested in British and in Foreign India, where they are now almost entirely abolished.

The establishment of a perfectly free port to the Northward as for instance at Chusan would tend to counteract these restrictions; the Chinese junks when out of sight of their own ports and unwatched would freely purchase goods* which the native traders would through various

*Since the above was penned, the "Hong Kong Register", a journal belonging to Messrs. Jardine, Matheson & Co., contains in an editorial

channels carry into the interior without the Chinese custom house stamp, which renders goods prohibitory or which is an incitement to extortions at the different transit stations.

Irrespective of the value which I have endeavoured to demonstrate in my "report on Chusan" of the military and naval advantages, and of the geographical position of that island, its intrinsic worth as a station for expanded commerce is unquestionable, and the large number of peaceful inhabitants engaged in husbandry on Chusan and on the neighboring islands is in itself an advantage for the promotion of our trade.

On the Fourth point viz; the cession of a barren, unhealthy, and useless rock at the Southern extremity of the Empire is almost unnecessary to offer a comment, as few disinterested persons now deny that a great error was committed by our acceptance of Hong Kong. Time and events have confirmed the accuracy of my "Report" upon the Island; it is still devoid of trade and without prospect of any native or European traffic; its insalubrity is beyond a doubt, * its inapplicability for colonization, unfortunate geographic position even as regards the Canton River estuary and its inappropriateness as a military station for the maintenance of British Supremacy in China are now pretty generally acknowledged; and many who have spent large sums in building under the delusion that Hong Kong would become a commercial emporium would be glad to get back even a moiety of their outlay.

article of 15th April 1845, the following remarks: "A great many new houses and shops are building at Chusan, and a much larger number of boats and Junks now frequent the harbour". Had we permanent possession of Chusan, it would be difficult to define the limit to which our influence in China and our trade to Shantung, the north of China, Korea, and perhaps even to Japan might extend either in British or in native bottoms.

*During the year 1843 the deaths among the troops at Hong Kong were 1 in three and a half; in Chusan one in 29 and a half. By official returns printed in the "Friend of China" of 16 April 1845, it appears that the mortality of 1844 has been dreadful: on an average strength of 1800 men the deaths were 373 and the invaliding was 333, a total of 706, equal to one third of the garrison! The survivors were unequal to one heavy day's march. Among the deaths were seven European Officers, among the invalidings twelve European Officers. Of 6 Officers who lived at Chusan for 18 months, not one died or invalided, and the troops are in as perfect health as if they were in England.

The Supplemental Treaty which throughout was framed restrictively and adversely to British interests* destroyed the only chance however remote that Hong Kong had of even being a resort for junks from the coast. The treaty was however almost superrogatory, for natural and insuperable difficulties prevent the island ever being made worthy the name of a British Colony. On a summary review of the past+, it would appear that we have not derived the fair and legitimate advantages we had a right to obtain from the recent war, and that as usual we have lost by diplomacy the position which had been gained by the sword.

1. In money we have not been reimbursed for the expenditure incurred during the war, and we are still incurring a very heavy and unprofitable outlay on this coast.

2. The expected advantages from opening four commercial ports in addition to the Port of Canton have not been realized; we are still restricted in our intercourse locally and generally, and life and property are considered by no means secure at Canton itself, within a hundred yards of the British Factory. Ingress is still denied to the City of Canton, where the people are encouraged to treat us with marked contumely and insult, accompanied in some instances by robbery and violence within sight of the city walls.

3. The reduction of the duties on commerce and of the Port charges on small coasting craft and the regulations respecting junks trading with Hong Kong require further modification and a satisfactory arrangement with reference to internal transit duties, which latter is particularly essential if Chusan be not made a free port or be not permanently retained as one of our colonies.

4. The cession of Hong Kong to the British Crown was no gain in any one point of view for England; on the contrary, its occupation has caused a great destruction of valuable life and considerable waste of treasure, while the retention of the island even with the most rigid economy must involve an annual sacrifice unattended with any beneficial results. We made no arrangement for the revision of the Treaty at the end of 7 or 10 years, when the working of its provisions would have been tested by time and experience, and we made no stipulations for the protection of those professing the Christian Faith. Both these

*H.M. Plenipotentiary who framed this treaty now declares that he was "an umpire" between Britain and China. It was supposed that he was sent here for the protection and advancement of British interests.

+The Prohibition of vessels from Hong Kong alone going beyond the 32° of N. Latitude has not been adverted to, the injustice, impolicy and unnationality being so obvious. Such an edict emanating from the Court of Peking seems quite consistent, but that it should be formed by a British Plenipotentiary seems quite incredible.

points were conceded to the Americans and French as soon as asked, and we are indebted to foreigners for concessions that ought to have been obtained by ourselves.

Having briefly reviewed the past, it may now be enquired what is our present position and policy? Do we feel secure of continued peace with China? Do we possess any commanding political position the retention of which by a moderate naval and military force may arrest the direful calamity of another war? Have we any check to exercise over the Chinese which may compell them to keep peace? Are we developing by precept or example any moral control or influence which may surely though slowly establish our power and win the respect and attachment of the Chinese Government and people? These important questions cannot, it is to be feared, be answered in the affirmative. The frequent expression of men of all classes of society is, "Another war with China is inevitable; affairs are not yet settled."

On the evacuation of Chusan, we shall have no position in China capable of dictating peace, and by the final abandonment of that island in January next, we shall have adopted the most effectual step that could be taken for the encouragement of a bloody and perhaps disastrous conflict, of which it is impossible to foresee the termination, and which it is very probable may engender deep and bitter feelings of national hostility to us, unquenchable by time or circumstances. As a Government we are doing nothing for the inculcation of our language, or for rearing a corps of useful and honest interpreters, European or Chinese; we are not merely negative but prohibitory as regards the dissemination of true religion, although there is no point on which the Chinese Government and people are more indifferent; and on other points we are equally unmindful of our permanent interests.

Painful however as it is to contemplate the mistakes of the past policy and the defects of our present position, there is much to cheer and encourage the efforts of the statesman if efficient measures be vigorously and promptly adopted for their remedy.

Our mistakes appear to have had their origin in a misplaces leniency and in the manifestation of a magnanimity which was misunderstood and which conveyed no real and permanent benefit on the conquered. A proud and corrupt Government like that of China inflated with the highest ideas of self-importance viewed honorable and humane concessions as indications of timidity or folly, and where it could not oppose force by force, it would naturally resort to the weapons of the weak: dissimulation, cunning, and perfidy.

When therefore we found ourselves the victors of China, it was our duty, while carefully abstaining from doing aught to diminish the control of the Chinese Government over its subjects, to have adopted such measures and to have taken such precautions as would have prevented the grievous necessity of another war by retaining an island or position as a guarantee which would command peace, by the establishment of a permanent British embassy at Peking, and by securing perfect freedom of intercourse for British subjects with every part of China internal or maritime. This would have been sound policy and at the same time merciful towards both the Chinese Government and people. The former would probably be saved the disastrous calamity of another war which may end in the subversion of the ruling dynasty, and the latter as an imitative and tractable people would have received the great and numerous benefits of unrestricted communion with a more civilized nation capable of turning to full advantage the qualities of an industrious and peaceable race in a country improved by art and favored by nature in a high degree. In order therefore to accomplish the important objects which it appears desirable should be attained by England for the sake of China as well as for our own interests, the following points are submitted for consideration:

1. The final cession of Chusan to the British Crown.
   a. Failing this cession, the island to be placed under the protection of Great Britain like the Ionian islands.
   b. This not being granted, Chusan to be made a Free Port open to all nations, with perfect freedom of residence &c.
2. In consideration of the Chinese ceding Chusan to England, we might agree to withdraw our Consular stations from Amoy, Foochow, and perhaps from Ningpo.
3. If the Chinese Government refuse to cede Chusan, then we ought to demand the permanent establishment of a British minister at Peking with a guard of honor, from a Ship of War to be constantly stationed in the Pei Ho, and that all official intercourse be carried on at Peking.
4. We ought also to require that British subjects be permitted to reside in any part of China with perfect security for life and property, for the free enjoyment of their religion and for the prosecution of any lawful and proper business.
5. That other ports be opened to British commerce, viz: those in the Yangtze Kiang river and to the Northward, and that it be permitted us to navigate any rivers in China.
6. That one of the other islands of the Chusan group, viz; the populous and cultivated island of Lowang, 26 miles in circumference, or the island of Tehinsanna, 8 and a half miles long from East to West with good anchorages in both monsoons, on the northeast parts of the Chusan group or archipelago [conclusion of sentence omitted in original, -- ed.]

By the adoption of such a system of definite policy, we should be establishing a physical and moral power in China of the utmost consequence to us as a nation an pregnant with beneficial results of the highest magnitude. It is the duty of statesmen to legislate and act for the future as well as for the present. The prescient mind can discern in the vista of coming events, a period when the peninsula of Hindustan will claim that right of self-government for which we are now educating the

the Anglo-Indian people. We ought to be preparing for such a change and to be now engaged in the formation of a controlling and directing power in China which will compensate for our loss in India, in somewhat the same manner as India compensated for our loss in the United States. China in a remarkable degree seems destined by Divine Providence to be the next great arena for the development of British civilization. The vast extent of territory favored by every variety of climate and yielding almost every vegetable and mineral product, the great length of sea coast with numerous excellent harbours, the large rivers flowing far and deep into the central land, abundance of coal and iron for steam navigation and transit, canals for traffic in all directions, a population numbering it is said one-third of the inhabitants of the earth, industrious, peaceful, skilled in husbandry and various branches of art, imitative in mechanics (thus leading to the natural conclusion that they would be equally so in social and moral duties), having an organized Government and well-administered municipalities, devoid of the prejudices of caste or of idolatry, and thus to a certain degree prepared for the reception of the seeds of Christian Truth, ever seeking to benefit their condition by labour at home or by emigrating to other countries, habituated to a maritime life, of considerable physical power, not deficient in courage if properly disciplined, acute or subtle reasoners, preferring the material to the theoretical or ideal, not wanting in imitative enterprise, obedient to the commands of a justly ruling authority, and with strong domestic and social attachments, enabling them to combine for good or evil purposes: -- these and other considerations render China a field peculiarly well adapted for the inculcation of the Christian civilization of England.

We have it in our power to till the field thus presented for our profitable labour. Science and skill of various kinds is now anxiously seeking employment at home; where could they be more usefully employed than in China?

Russia, Turkey, Greece, Belgium, Egypt, Persia and other countries have been benefitted by the scientific skill of Europe; here is a region open to us for the same purpose, far exceeding in value and in extent all those kingdoms put together. If we refuse to avail ourselves of the offer thus benignly vouchsafed to us, if we reject the means of benefitting ourselves and myriads of our fellow creatures,either from apathy, selfishness, miscalled prudence, or erroneous political considerations, the opportunity may never again occur, and that which might have been converted into a source of national strength, of individual good, and of general benefit may be converted by others and by different means into an engine injurious to our interests, and productive of great and permanent national injury. Are we prepared to run the race of competition with other nations? Or after enjoying duration as a kingdom for upwards of one thousand years, and holding for the greater part of that time the dominant Power of the Earth, are we disposed to shrink from the competition and descend in the scale of Empires? Other Kingdoms and Nations are ready to rise, to build, and to strengthen their power on our downfall. We cannot shut our eyes to the fact that we are envied and feared rather than trusted and loved, and that if we be not true to ourselves there are none in whom we can trust.

It has not been by a timid, hesitating, dubious, time-serving policy, by a craving after petty immediate gain, by crafty devices or by subtle intrigues, that a small island in the western Atlantic has become the mistress of the World, her power seen and felt on every shore, her flag triumphant on every sea. Great ends can only be achieved by great means, a nobility of object consecrates the noble deeds for its attainment.

If to pour a quickening life blood into China, to vivify a vast and almost stagnant mass of human beings and thus incalculably increase our commerce, if to construct and organise a Power on the Extreme East which may eventually counterbalance the gigantic Empire which stretches from the Bosphorus to the Artic circle, from the Baltic to the Pacific, if to diffuse intelligence and science among three hundred millions of people, above all and before all to implant the inspiriting doctrines of Christianity over such an immense portion of the globe that their diffusion would eventually influence all mankind, if to do this be worthy the achievement of Britain, and that even failure in the attempt be no disgrace, but the reverse, then ought we to proceed very differently from the course which has hitherto been adopted; nay more, a perseverance in our present course can bring with it no advantage, it will not even obtain security for our tea trade, although the Chinese are more interested in preserving that branch of commerce than the English are; and when war and anarchy have overspread and desolated China, we shall find when too late that we have lost even that for which we had vainly forfeited every individual and national good.

It is yet time to retrieve some of the errors of the past. Ere Chusan be evacuated in January next, we have the means in our power of arranging those measures which wisdom, mercy to China, and sound policy to ourselves would dictate. Some of those measures have been briefly shadowed forth in the previous pages, and can if required be more amply developed. Happy will the writer feel if in the fulfilment of his duty to his Sovereign he has been permitted to aid in awakening Britain to a true sense of her positon in China, to a consciousness of what is due to herself and at the same time beneficial to others, and to a strenuous effort for maintaining a National Supremacy in the East as well as in the West which is essentially conducive to the welfare of all mankind.

CANTON CONSULATE
RECORDS CONCERNING
THE LANDS AND TENEMENTS AT
HONAN

British Consulate Canton
23 April 1847

Copy David Jardine Esq.
Chairman of the British
Chamber of Commerce

Sir,

In consequence of the instructions received from Her Majesty's Plenipotentiary and Superintendent of Trade, I have lately had several interviews with the Mandarins on the subject of the lands and tenements at Honan.

From what they state it appears that the space set apart for British subjects belongs to several proprietors who have let the grounds to a great number of small tenants for the cultivation of rice &c. These latter live in a village on the spot and naturally are averse to parting with their houses and lands, from the former of which according to local custom they cannot be ejected so long as they continue to pay the rent. There will be probably less difficulty as respects the warehouses and other buildings on the river as they are in the hands of a limited number of people belonging to a different class from the occupiers of the lands.

In order to facilitate the negotiations, I had proposed that the whole tract within the limits constituted by the river, the Macao passage, and the creek, should be surveyed by an Engineer; this has not, however, been decreed expedient for the present, on the ground that it might irritate the villagers and give rise to disturbances.

I have confined myself therefore to demand of the mandarins a plan of the locality in question, shewing the several parcels of ground, the names of the Proprietors, the nature of the principal buildings, and indicating the public roads.

I transmit this plan enclosed such as it is, and I only regret that it does not specify the measure of the several parcels of land and of the numerous fishponds, except in a singular instance where the lands to the eastward of the road, intersecting the plan from north to south and belonging to the Pwan Family, is stated at 133 mou, equal to about 28 English miles. If these data be correct, the superficies of the whole space (not including the building grounds) would be between 50 and 60 acres, as it was estimated on our first impression.

It being highly desirable for obvious reasons that the matter should be simplified as much as circumstances permit, I have to request with reference to the preceding plan, that all those who wish to avail themselves of the advantages secured to British subjects by Her Majesty's Plenipotentiary and Superintendent of Trade should indicate on the map and transmit to me with all convenient speed a written application for such lands and tenements as they are desirous of acquiring by lease or by purchase, in order that either by direct negotiations with the proprietors or tenants, or through the instrumentality of the mandarins, an arrangement with the parties may be brought about on the most moderate terms.

In conclusion, I beg to add for your information that according to the standard length of the chang used for measuring land, which has been communicated to me by the assistant magistrate of Nanhae, the chang is equal to 146 1/2 inches, hence 4.07 mou are equal to one English acre of 43,560 square feet.

From this information I have collected concerning the value and rent of land in this vicinity, I am enabled to state that the Land at Honan is worth from 95 to 110 dollars per mou on an average, that portion situated most favourable for irrigation being more valuable than grounds distant from the river. This price does not include, however, the patches of dry building ground but refers merely to the ponds and paddy fields.

The annual rent constitutes about 6 per cent upon the price, the proprietors paying the Imperial land tax. Hence taking the average price of the whole space (exclusive of building ground) at $100 per mou, the annual rent would be $29.22 or 126/g sterling per English acre.

I have &c.

(signed)
Francis C. Mac Gregor

A Statement of such lands and tenements as have been applied for at Her Majesty's Consulate at Canton between the 24th April and 7th May inclusive, by the individuals undermentioned, viz. (1847)

Date of application	No.	Name of applicant	Object applied for: Warehouses	Object applied for: Lands	Where situated
April 24	1	David Jardine	Houses	Lands	On the point formed by the Main River and the Macao passage branch
April 24	2	J. Larkins	Warehouses	"	In front of the Main River and adjoining the lot applied for by Mr. Jardine
May 3	3	Crooke & Massey	"	"	To the South of Mr. Jardine's lot in the Macao passage
May 3	4	Gilman & Co.	"	"	Above the Fort Rouge and below Mr. Spencer Compton's lot
May 5	5	"	"	& Lands	In the Macao passage beyong certain sheds contiguous to Mr. C.S. Compton's lot
May 6	6	Charles S. Compton	"	"	Bounded on the West by the Macao passage and on the South by Mr. Gilman's lot
May 6	7	British Community	"	All lands	Within the embankments not at present occupied by buildings or roads
May 6	8	Murrow & Co.	"	"	Facing the main river, between Mr. C.S. Compton's lot and Mr. Walker's
May 6	9	Dirom, Gray & Co.	"	"	Between Fort Rouge and the Western extremity of the building facing the main river
May 6	10	Charles Ryder	Sheds	"	Bounded West by the Macao Passage, South by the creek, West & East by Paddy fields
May 6	11	Mac Vicar & Co.	Warehouses	"	To the Eastward of the Fort Rouge on the River, being the 4 and 5 Warehouses
May 7	12	Alexander Walker	"	"	Facing the Main River between Murrow & Co's and J. Larkins'

Extract from Dispatch No. 47 of 9th May.1947, from Mr. Consul Macgregor to Sir John Davis

With respect to the Lands and houses at Honan, I enquired of the Mandarins what steps they had taken since I had at the last meeting pointed out to them on the plan the three Lots applied for by Mr. Jardine, Captain Larkins, and Messrs. Crooke and Massey, requiring them to procure from the owners a statement of the rents of the different buildings &c., on these lots. The Mandarins in answer said that as yet they had not succeeded in inducing such of the proprietors as were known to them to enter into any negotiation, nor had they been able to find out all the proprietors of the land.

The ground applied for up to this present day (of which I forwarded to Your Excellency an abstract in my Dispatch No 46) was then pointed out to them on the plan furnished by themselves exhibiting one compact piece of ground, bounded on the North by the main River, towards the West by a small creek (not on the map) connected with the two branches of the river already mentioned. I called upon the mandarins to furnish me with a specifications of the rents demanded by the different proprietors for the whole of this property, and also of the prices of the buildings and tenements erected on that portion of it which is situated in from off the river, some of the merchants being desirous to purchase their lots.

The mandarins eventually agreed to procure these details, but not until they had repeatedly pressed on me to induce the merchants to negotiate with the proprietors through the compradores, in which case they would furnish a list of the former. They alleged that if they themselves inquired concerning the prices and rents of the lands and houses claimed by foreigners, a settlement would be attended with much greater difficulties than if the merchants' compradors were employed for that purpose. As their object, however, evidently was to throw all the trouble, odium, and responsibility of the measure upon us, I distinctly told them that as on the one hand I had procured definite offers and applications from the British merchants, so on the other hand it was incumbent upon them to ascertain from the Chinese proprietors what prices or rents they demanded in order to arrive at the real value of the objects to be ceded to British subjects by the late agreement. But the passive resistance of the people in this Province to all measures in favour of Foreigners, combined with the little power which the Mandarins can exercise on such occasions, are serious obstables in the way of a speedy completion of the proposed arrangement, and if the same object was attained with comparative ease at Shanghai it must be remembered that the Mandarins there have preserved a greater degree of influence over the people, who are of a more phlegmatic temperament and less prejudiced against Foreigners than they are and always have been at Canton.

British Consulate Canton
No 79 26th May 1847

Sir,

In conformity with the wishes expressed in Your Excellency's No. 66, I did not delay in calling upon the British Merchants to convene a meeting in order to express their sense in regard to the Honan locality under the circumstances of the objections on the part of the proprietors, and to make propositions as to any substitute.

A meeting of the British merchants was held in consequence this morning, and I have the honor of transmitting to Your Excellency enclosed a copy of the resolutions which were there passed.

It is the opinion of the merchants that the demand of the locality at Honan made by Your Excellency, and granted by the Imperial Commissioner in terms of the Treaty, should be at once enforced, unless a more desirable site can be obtained; but that the objections of the Gentry and Elders in their letter to me of the 20th (which I forwarded to Your Excellency yesterday by an Extra Boat) are altogether inadmissable, since the same objections would be raised with additional force by proprietors elsewhere if allowed to be valid in this instance.

They further consider it to be of the utmost consequence to the interests of the trade that this important question be immediately settled, as business, which now is almost entirely at a stand, cannot be expected to improve until not only the people of Canton but all connected with its trade are fully assured that our relations with China are placed on a more satisfactory footing. As regards my own opinion upon the subject, I consider it a precedent fraught with evil to allow the people to combine, as they have done on the present occasion, for the purpose of frustrating any of the objects of the Treaty concluded between our Government and their own; but if it should be determined upon to give up the plan of acquiring the lands of Honan, in consideration of the difficulties encountered by the local authorities in disposing the people to lease them to British subjects, I am inclined to think that this can only consistently be done on the following conditions, viz:

1. That the proposal for such commutation emanuates from the local authorities.

2. That the local authorities assign to us and put us in possession of another tract of land of about 50 acres if possible at a similar distance from Canton.

At the same time, the Honan proprietors of warehouses and building grounds on the river should be firmly bound by their own authorities to discontinue any combination tending to prevent us from leasing these houses and grounds at fair and reasonable rates, to be agreed upon between the parties, under the mediation if required of the British Consul and the local authorities.

The proprietors of such tenements, however, at the same time, ought to be told that if they obstinately continue to combine for the purpose of frustrating the fulfillment of the 7th article of the Treaty, their Emperor will justly be displeased with their perverse conduct, which ultimately may draw great calamity upon themselves and their families.

I have &c.

(signed)
Francis C. Macgregor

Extract

Copy of Resolutions agreed to at a Public meeting of the British community held in the rooms of the Canton British Chamber of Commerce, on the 26th May 1847. Present 71 persons, David Jardine in the chair.

1. That an adequate space of land on Honan for the use of the British community have been demanded by Her Majesty's Plenipotentiary, and granted by the Imperial Commissioner in terms of the Treaty, it is the opinion of this meeting that such demand should be at once enforced, unless a more desirable site can be obtained, and that the objections raised by the Gentry and Elders in their letter to H. M. Consul of 20 Inst. are altogether inadmissable, since the same objections apply equally to all lands in China, and would certainly be brought forward, and urged with additional force by proprietors elsewhere, if admitted to be valid in this instance.

2. That this meeting is not at present prepared to suggest a more eligible site than granted at Honan; its proximity to the present foreign factories, its large extent of river frontage, and the open space of ground available for exercise, rendering it more suitable to our wants than any other spot in this neighborhood, and if any other place is offered by the Chinese authorities in its stead, this meeting trusts that the British community will be made acquainted with its locality, and be afforded an opportunity of communicating their sentiments regarding it, before final arrangements are made.

British Consulate
Canton 28 May 1847

No. 81

Sir,

In conformity with the instructions conveyed by Your Excellency's dispatch No. 68 to ascertain the views of the British merchants as to the suitability of Whampoa as a place of recreation, I requested Mr. Jardine to convene a meeting to that effect which was held this morning and where a Resolution was passed from which it appears that, in the opinion of the British Residents, Whampao is too far distant from Canton to be suitable either as a place of recreation or business, and further that nothing has occurred to alter the opinion expressed at the meeting of the 26th instant, that the acquisition of the site of ground at Honan as per 4th Article of the new agreement should be enforced.

*** *** *** *** *** *** ***

I have &c.

(signed)
Francis C. Macgregor

No. 99

British Consulate
Canton 10 June 1847

Sir,

In Your Excellency's No. 83, I find a passage quoted from my dispatch No. 91 in which I remarked on informing you of two packhouses having been offered by the proprietors at Honan that I doubted people would be inclined to rent packhouses there so long as the question about the lease of the Paddy ground in the rear of these tenements had not been decided in our favour.

I think it right to state to Your Excellency in explanation that my doubts chiefly arose from the consideration that if any numbers of our merchants were located at Honan without the land in their rear having previously been secured, the places contiguous to their dwellings would immediately be occupied and built upon by the Chinese who are always inclined to establish themselves in the vicinity of the foreigners, in expectation of deriving some advantage or other from it in their traffic with them. Besides being prevented to extend their buildings in the rear, the merchants would be exposed to additional risk in case of fire from the proximity of Chinese houses and sheds. I do not believe therefore that any disinclination they may now shew to lease houses at Honan originates merely in a spirit of opposition, nor do I find on examination that the number of applicants for allotments increased the moment that any obstacles arose, it being on record that out of nineteen applications, sixteen were made between the 24th April and 15th May, whereas no opposition on the part of the Chinese to our having land at Honan manifested itself until the 20th May, the date of the address of the Gentry and Elders.

I have &c.

(signed)
Francis C. Macgregor

Extract from dispatch No. 107 of 15 June 1847 from Mr. Consul Macgregor to Sir John Davis

The Mandarins further delivered to me the particulars about the Packhouses on the other side of the creek, namely

1.	The Tienpaou Hong 2nd East from the creek	Rent 6000 taels
2.	The Tungshun Hong 3rd East from the creek	Rent 6000 taels
3.	The Tungfow Hong lately occupied by Mr. Jardine	Rent 2400 taels

but as rent demanded seems to be enormous as compared with that of other packhouses, I observed to the mandarins that unless it were reduced according to the present standard of prices I did not think it likely that any of them would be taken.

I then reverted to the subject of lands at Honan to the extent of fifty acres stipulated for by the fourth section of the late agreement. From the arguments used by the mandarins on this subject I gathered that they understood, from the tenor of several phrases in your late declarations to the people of Honan, that these latter should not be molested if unwilling to lease their ground to us, and that Honan was not the only place on the river, but that other places between this and Whampoa might be made available for the purpose of being leased. From this they inferred that you had given up the grounds at Honan, and that the question was only to point out another locality. I told them, however, that they were mistaken, inasmuch as that the fourth article was in full force, and that its execution would be insisted on unless they, the mandarins, were prepared to offer another space equally suitable which hitherto they had not done. They replied that they had not been remiss in making enquiries, but that they had experienced great difficulty in finding any tract of land on the river in the immediate vicinity of the town unoccupied; they added, however, that they had their eyes upon two eligible places in this neighborhood, where they hoped to be able to procure land for the British merchants.

The one is to the east of the city, being one of the islets formed by the river, where it separates into two large and one or two small passages, just below the French Folly. According to the plan the mandarins shewed me, it seemed to be the most southerly of these islets. Distance about three miles.

The other place lies to the northwest of the city near the Fahte gardens. It is on the north side of the passage to Fuhshan, which passes the Fahte Gardens. Area about twelve acres. Distance about one and a half miles.

British Consulate
Canton 23 June 1857 (sic)

No. 116

Sir,

The mandarins "Tung" and "Ning" have just left me, but I am sorry to say that since our last meeting, no progress whatever has been made with respect to the houses and lands at Honan and elsewhere.

Regarding the tenements at Honan, they declared that "Chin", the proprietor of the five packhouses there, to whom they had applied in order to obtain his consent for erecting a dwelling house on the premises for the accommodation of Messrs. Crooke and Massey, had refused it, alleging that although willing to lease his packhouses, he would not allow foreigners to build and reside on his grounds. As on the one hand Messrs. Crooke and Massey do not seem to have any use for the packhouses without a dwelling house, and as on the other, the proprietor cannot be compelled to allow the erection of new buildings on his grounds, I conceive that the negotiation between the parties must be considered as broken off, unless Messrs. Crooke and Massey change their minds.

On my representing to the mandarins that the rents demanded for the Hongs on the other side of the creek were out of proportion, as compared with those prevailing among the people, they promised to exert themselves to the utmost of their power in order to obtain a reduction in price from the proprietors, who belong to the old Hong merchants, which I presume will not be difficult as they are all more or less heavily indebted to the Chinese Government.

They have not concluded their negotiations with the proprietor of the land to be offered to our merchants near the Fahte Gardens, in consequence of some discussion having arisen with the farmer, who is unwilling to give up his lease; but they assured me that they will do their best to bring the matter to a speedy settlement, and inform me of the result. Having inspected the farm myself a few days ago, I have reason to think that it would be well adapted for a place of recreation, although not for purposes of business, on account of its distance from town.

I have &c.

(signed)
Francis C. Macgregor

Copy of a Placard which was posted on 24th June 1847 at the North End of Old China Street warning the proprietors of the land near the Fahte Gardens against renting their grounds to foreigners.

At present the High Authorities and the English Officers mutually adhere to the treaties formerly concluded. In all of these it is declared that the property of the people may not be forcibly taken possession of, whence it follows that in the treaties the studied intention is to have full consideration for the feelings of the people, and not to give them any annoyance. Now we have heard that the Nanking branch of the Pwan family in Honan has some property situated at the entrance to the Shan village, the local name of which is Shih wei tang, which they at the instigation of certain traitors at length desire to sell to the Barbarians.

It is in our opinion extremely contrary to the principles of benevolence for the Nanking branch of the Pwan family, who have refused to make over their property at Honan to the Barbarians to wish on the contrary to make it over to them only in our neighborhood and thereby prevent the people of several tens of our villages from taking pleasure in their occupations and living in quiet.

Further, Shih wei tang is the general road for intercourse between Canton, Foshan and the North and West Rivers, and the banks of the river are inhabited by husbandmen, the fields and houses being in connection, which is different from vacant land and empty houses. From this it may be perceived that the High Authorities do not wish to give nor the English officers to take it. Again it appears from the replies of the English officers to the gentry and Elders of Honan that they wish the Chinese and Barbarians to treat each other with politeness; how then can our people of Kwangtung bear to contract enmity with them?

At present a noise and clamour is raised in the villages and alarm and fear has spread far and near. Should therefore the Nanking branch of the Pwan family ultimately sell their property to the Barbarians, it must under the circumstances lead to disturbances, and what advantage is there in a number of people contracting enmity on account of one proprietor.

Further the inhabitants of the Paous* of the adjoining townships and the people going to and from the mart of Foshan five loud utterance to annoying language, which we are not able to repeat in detail; but if disturbances should one break out it will be impossible for you to bear the anger of the public, from which one or two intelligent people will not be able to rescue you. We respectfully give you this information.

A public Notification of the inhabitants of the whole township in the neighborhood of Shih wei tang.

* Paou is the subdivision of a sze or township

Postscript.

In the Nanking branch of the Pwan family there is the Hong merchant Pwan Shao-kuang and various elders who are quite able to arrange this matter. Should they, however, slight us, the inhabitants of the Paou, in general, by secretly receiving a price for their property and making over the latter to the Barbarians, the Nanking branch of the Pwan family shall be responsible for it.

(No date.)

A true translation
(signed) Thos. Taylor
Meadows
(Interpreter)

Note. The "Postscript" was on a small piece of paper posted by the side of the placard at the North end of Old China Street.

(signed) T. T. M.

No. 12 Canton 1st July 1847

Notice issued by Mr. Consul Macgregor to the British Mercantile community

Notice is hereby given to such of Her Majesty's subjects as may be desirous of hiring dwellings or warehouses under the provisions of Section 7 of the Supplementary Treaty, that the Local authorities have assigned for that purpose the following tenements in the places and at the respective rents undermentioned, namely:

A. In the suburb called Honan

1. a plot of ground on the Macao passage, and containing the following buildings, viz.:

	Rent demanded
The Fuh-tseang Packhouse	280 taels
The Tung-yang "	450 "
The Shin-tseang "	450 "
The Hwung ke "	220 "
The Paou chin "	130 "
Total rent	1330 taels

per annum in half-yearly installments, the rent being paid in advance on possession being given of the premises.

2. A space of ground fronting the main river, and containing the following buildings, viz.:

	Rent demanded per annum
A packhouse being the last in the line extending to the West of the Red Fort	1600 taels
A packhouse at the back of the preceding	600 "
Total	2200 taels

Possession will be given to the lessees after a certain lapse of time to make the necessary alterations for dwelling places in the respective premises mentioned under Nos. 1 & 2.

B. In the Southern Suburb

The following tenements situate on the river in a line extending from the creek to the Eastward of the new factories have been offered at the following reduced rates, viz.:

1. The Teen paou Hong, containing in all ten subdivisions or compartments; the rent demanded for each of which is 600 dollars additional for each of the two back compartments nearest the river, which have an upper storey. Total rent demanded for the Hong per annum -- 7200 dollars.
2. The Tungshun Hong, containing ten compartments, two of which (nearest the river) have upper stories. The rent for each compartment (600 dollars) is the same as for the Teen paou Hong. Total rent demanded for the Hong per annum -- 7200 dollars.
3. The Tung fou Hong, containing ten compartments but without upper floors to any of them. Rent demanded for each compartment -- 600 dollars. Total rent for the Hong per annum -- 6000 dollars.
4. In the Quang le Hong, the two compartments nearest the river, which have upper stories, and are at present vacant. Rent demanded for each compartment -- 1200 dollars, and for both -- 2400 dollars.

Persons wishing to rent any of the respective tenements before mentioned or any portion thereof are requested to make application for the same at the British Consulate, where the necessary steps will be taken for placing them in communication with the proprietors, and for bringing about an arrangement between the parties.

No. 13

Ke, Imperial Commissioner, Governor General of the Two Kwangs... &c.,...&c.,...&c. hereby gives a declaration in reply to the representation of Koo Lau Yung, and others.

After examination I find that an Imperial Edict was a long time back respectfully received permitting foreign merchants to dwell at the ports open to foreign commerce and stating that the lands and houses to be rented by them should be determined by the inclination or otherwise of the proprietors to let. It cannot therefore in any way concern other people that Pwan She-lee is now inclined to give up his patrimonial property of Shih wei tang for the use of Government. You have represented that "the foreigners will stealthily take possession of the upper streams, seize the most important passages, settle on the most important places, inflict bitter injuries on the villages, &c.". This is of course in consequence of your having listened to and being moved by idle reports. You should reflect that the whole tract of country in the vicinity of this city is important and that it is not Shih wei tang alone which is so. Further, Shih wei tang does not lie at any distance from the Thirteen factories, the inhabitants in the neighborhood of which have for a long time past had peace and tranquility; why then should your several tens of villages forthwith suffer bitter injury?

Having had the honor to receive a Commission from His Imperial Majesty to take the management of all affairs between Chinese and foreigners, and having in all matters reverently received His Sacred instructions, my object is to put a stop to troubles, and to tranquilize the people, without in the slightest degree entertaining my selfish views.

You, being all people advanced in years, ought, I conceive, to possess a thorough knowledge of affairs, and not allow yourselves to be deluded by idle tales.

A paper annexed to the original representation.

Published officially on the 5th of July 1847.

A true translation.
(signed)
Thos. Taylor Meadows
(interpreter)

No. 14

British Chamber of Commerce
Canton 5 July 1847

Sir,

I have the honor of acknowledging receipt of your letter of the 1st July, enclosing copy of a notice addressed to the British mercantile community of Canton offering on the part of the Chinese Local Authorities certain tenements on Hire as dwellings or warehouses under the provisions of Article VII of the Supplementary Treaty. This notice has been laid before the British community and parties desirous of availing themselves of the Buildings offered will communicate with you direct on the subject.

While thanking you for this communication and expressing on the part of the Chamber of Commerce the satisfaction with which they observe in the offer now made, a disposition to carry out the terms of the Treaty and the obligations of the arrangement entered into between His Excellency Her Majesty's Plenipotentiary and the Imperial Commissioner in April last, I am directed to remark that isolated spots in distant and scattered situations cannot afford to the Mercantile Community the advantages promised under the management alluded to, deprived, as parties occupying such property would be, of the comfort and security afforded by proximity of residence one to another.

Francis C. Macgregor Esquire
at B. M. Consul Canton

No. 15

British Consulate
Canton 15 July 1847

No. 139

Sir,

Since my last report I have had another meeting with the mandarins Tung and Ning who called yesterday and delivered to me the particulars about the place called Shih wei tang, for which, if purchased, the sum of eight thousand Taels is demanded by the possessor of the ground, independently of twenty thousand taels which the present occupant asks for the buildings erected, the plantation laid out, and for other improvements made during the thirty years that he has been living on the Farm, which is stated to contain about 70 Mow or 15 acres. In the event of its being leased, the annual rent demanded is 2300 Taels, subject perhaps to a trifling reduction.

The enclosed is a specification of the buildings and tenements, plantations, and fish ponds on the Farm, to which I added a statement of the annual Revenue derived from each of these objects in particular. Although the rent would appear extremely high as compared with the small extent of the ground, yet the Mandarins expressed it as their conviction that the above estimates had been made on a moderate computation and being considered as a set off against the rent, the annual expense of the place itself would be but trifling.

I shall not fail to make the necessary communication on the subject of this farm to the merchants, and inform Your Excellency of the result in due time.

I have &c.
(signed)
Francis C. Macgregor

No. 16

British Consulate
Canton 3rd August 1847

No. 155

Sir,

I have the honor of reporting to Your Excellency that I have had an interview with the Chinese Commissioners Tung and Ning accompanied by Mr. Howqua for the purpose of settling the accounts regarding the purchase of the Six shops in Hogs Lane and the lease of the ground in the same locality to the British Community.

As to the second point Mr. Howqua has been appointed to draw up an indenture in the Chinese form, of the lease of the ground in Hogs Lane of which the superficial area as per measurement is 10,000 square feet, at the rate agreed upon of three cents per square foot, making three hundred dollars annual rent payable at the expiration of every six months -- the payment for the first six months falling due on the 31st December of the present year.

This business having been concluded I referred the Mandarins to the correspondence which had passed on the subject of the burial grounds at Whampoa stipulated for by the agreement of the 6th April and expressing to them at the same time my surprise that a matter of so little moment had not immediately been settled by them on the spot. They repeated all the arguments used by Ke ying in his letter to Your Excellency, but I observed to them that cemeteries had been granted to us by Treaty and that in particular the Parsees in whose favor the demand was made were obliged by their religious rites to assemble there at stated periods of the year to offer up prayers for their departed friends and that consequently the inclosure of the place was indispensable in order to avoid their being disturbed by the natives and that I must therefore insist upon the execution of this article of the Treaty without further delay. They then agreed to communicate with the Tepaou of the District on the subject and to exert themselves to the utmost to bring about a speedy and satisfactory arrangement.

I also showed them the necessity of a further reduction in the proposed rents of the three warehouses on the other side of the creek, and although at first they seemed little disposed to listen to my representations, they at last promised to make another effort with the proprietors of these tenements in inducing them to offer more equitable terms. With regard to Shih wei tang, I merely repeated what I already stated at my last interview with them considering it unnecessary to add anything more on the subject, the place being unsuitable both in point of distance and of price, besides which in the present excited state of the villagers it would be impossible to obtain quiet possession of it.

I have &c.
(signed)
Francis C. Macgregor

No. 17

British Chamber of Commerce
Canton August 5th 1847

Sir,

I have to apologise for not having sooner acknowledged the receipt of your letters of the 16th and 21st ultimo, the first acquainting me, for the information of the mercantile community, that the farm of Shih wei tang had been placed at the disposal of British residents by the Governor General of the Province, and the latter stating that the proprietor of the Kwang le Hong intended treating with other parties for the two compartments offered to British Residents if not availed of within ten days.

The contents of these letters were immediately made known to the British Community and they have since been laid before the Committee of this Chamber, who consider the farm of Shih wei tang at too great a distance from the Foreign Factories to be availed of either for Commercial purposes or for needful daily exercise and it is for these purposes that additional space is required. You are no doubt aware that the offer to let or sell this farm to foreigners has called forth an opposition on the part of the elders and gentry of that neighborhood hardly inferior to that of the Honan people on a late occasion. The walls of the principal thoroughfares are covered with abusive placards, directed against the grasping English Barbarians, and this is permitted in face of the recent notifications by the Chinese Authorities prohibiting such placards -- deputation after deputation has waited upon Keying and the owner of the ground; public meetings are being held day after day, at one of which it is understood it was resolved that certain buildings on the property which foreigners had been in the habit of occasionally visiting should be forcibly demolished if not immediately taken down of which notice was given to the owner, which has been obliged to have the objectionable buildings removed in deference of the wish of the gentry thus expressed. People from Foshan and the surrounding villages continue flocking to the spot. Foreigners have been refused permission to land, and very considerable excitement still prevails. This stir is only what was to be expected, and while the people are allowed to dictate to their Government, similar demonstrations, attended with the same results, must follow all attempts to obtain ground or any other concessions in favor of foreigners, who after four months' negotiation on this subject remain precisely where they were before, merely permitted to rent Packhouses and Hongs in various localities, widely sparated from each other. When this Committee had the honor of first bringing to your notice the great insecurity attending the management of business here, from the want of warehouse room connected with the dwellings of the merchants, they distinctly stated that Foreigners were at perfect liberty to rent packhouses where they pleased, but such buildings affording no accommodation for dwellings, property stored in them would still be left in the hands of Chinese, and which of course would not remedy the evil complained of. The Hongs have also been equally available to foreigners since the opening of the trade in 1843, without the intervention of Government, but if otherwise suitable, the enormous rents demanded place them beyond the reach of most of the merchants; they are besides little better than open sheds, built on low ground barely level with the river at high spring-tides, and liable to be flooded at certain periods of the year; they are not separated or detached, but closely wedged together, with a dense mass of buildings immediately in their rear, occupied chiefly be carpenters and other mechanics, and consequently much exposed to the risk of fire, against which risk property stored in them cannot be insured in China. If the ground upon which they stand were entirely cleared of buildings, or if any other vacant space conveniently situated could be obtained, it would be more valuable to

Foreigners than these Hongs, as two or at most three years rental, together with the outlay which would be required to make the best of them habitable for Europeans, would be ample for the erection of insurable buildings, sufficiently spacious perhaps for the requirements of the largest foreign establishment in the place. But if each ground cannot be obtained, and it is not deemed expedient to carry out a general measure in the manner contemplated by the 4th article of the New agreement, it would be much better that the merchants again be left to themselves, to make the best arrangements they can under the circumstances. The just alarm occasioned by the expedition four months ago, and the excitement since kept up by these fruitless negotiations, have done incalculable injury to the trade without bettering the position of Foreigners in the least, and it is exceedingly desirable that this ferment should now be permitted to subside.

Since writing the foregoing I have had the honor of receiving your letter of this date regarding the Hongs referred to in your letter of the 1st ultimo, which shall be immediately submitted to the British Community.

I have &c.
(signed) David Jardine

[Here follows a summary by Consul Harry Parkes of all the preceding correspondence, titled, "Memorandum Respecting Honan Land, From the Records of the Canton Consulate", concluding with this note, dated simply "August, 1847":]

The Chairman of the British Chamber of Commerce, objects to Shih wei tang as being too far removed from Canton, points out that it is building land and not Warehouses that they wish to be provided with, and that unless this can be obtained it would be better to leave them to make their own arrangements. "The negotiations," observes the Consul, "on these subjects with the Chinese Commissioners must I conceive therefore be considered at an end."

Harry S.Parkes
Consul of B. at Canton

THE MORRISON EDUCATION SOCIETY IN CHINA

4 May, 1848

This Society was originated in Canton in 1836, and it was named in honor of the late Dr. Morrison, D.D., the first Protestant Missionary to China, who furnished the most valuable key to the Chinese Language yet extant, and whose labours as a Missionary, Oriental Scholar, and Servant of his Government are so well known throughout Christendom: and it was formed with a view to carry out one branch of the great work to which he had devoted his life.

The object of the Institutuion is to establish and support schools in China, in which Native youths shall be taught in connection with their own the English language, so as to open to them the Stores of knowledge of which it is the repository and at the same time, by sound religious training and instruction, to raise them to the rank of enlightened Christian men. It is the belief of those most conversant with the state of things in this country that the hope of civilizing and evangelizing the Chinese can in no way be realized so speedily as by combining a rigorous system of educational efforts with the judiciary means of propagating the Gospel.

The agency to affect the masses of this populous empire, and to produce any great and desirable changes among a people so far civilized, but yet pagans, must be chiefly a native agency. To prepare this from among the young men of the country is the great aim of the Morrison Education Society. It does not propose to give them a professional education, but a general one, which shall serve to qualify them for the spheres of action for which they may be fitten whether by their abilities or their principles. To this end it has during the last eight years carried on its operations through a school, which since the Peace of 1842, has been established at Hong Kong.

Here native boys have been collected and while enjoying the privileges of a Christian family have, besides studying the Chinese, been particularly instructed in the English language through which they have been made acquainted with Western Science and History, but especially have learned to read the Sacred Scriptures and have been daily taught the way of life.

After this Institution, which is under the charge of the Reverend S.R. Brown (now temporarily absent in America for his health) and Mr. Macy, had been for some time established, it was determined by the Society that eight years should be the period for boys to remain under instruction, but prior to the opening of the School at Hong Kong in 1847, it was found impossible to carry out this system Regularly. The Parents of the children being unable to understand the motives of Foreigners thus wishing to educate and support their children, it was extremely difficult to induce them to remain at the Institution, and subsequently several of them left the School for various reasons after being only a short time there. Taking therefore these circumstances into consideration and at the same time that the school commenced with very few boys and has been but eight years in operation, it is not surprising that up to this time only six boys have gone through a course of education. Of these, two are now most usefully employed as Interpreters in the Government offices. One has gone to Shanghai to seek employment, and three of the most promising have gone with Mr. Brown, with a view of completing their Studies in England and America, and from the accounts lately received from that Gentleman, it appears they are going on most satisfactorily with every prospect of being, when they return to China, of essential service in furthering the object which this Society had in view. The numbers of boys now at the Institution is twenty-four.

Much valuable time is now devoted to teaching the boys their own language, and the elementary branches of education, which would be more profitably employed upon boys already possessing that knowledge, and evincing talent and aptitude for learning.

The Trustees are of opinion that the time has now arrived when this difficulty may be successfully met and overcome, and a most promising field of usefulness opened up in this colony by the establishment of one or more elementary schools under the immediate protection and control of the Society. At present there are only three Chinese Schools in the town of Victoria (exclusive of two or three supported and managed by Europeans) in which from 60 to 70 Children are taught a little reading and writing or occasional decimal computation on the Chinese counting board. The Teachers, however, are uneducated men and the instruction they give is consequently very defective.

The Parents of these Children allow the Teacher a small sum for each child, and the Government has for the last three months given a grant at the rate of $120 per annum. But there is a large number of children receiving no education whatever, and as regards the light of revealed religion, all remain in total darkness.

The number of Chinese boys under the age of 16 in Victoria alone amount to 725. Of English there are only 51, Portuguese 33, and Malays and Indians 35. Besides there are 600 boys living chiefly in boats here and at other parts of the Island.

The object the Trustees have in view is to educate in Chinese language and in Christian principles the Native youths of Hong Kong (not of course excepting those from other parts of China if they choose to repair to Hong Kong for this purpose) and to give in addition to those who desire it an elementary English education. The Chinese Teachers would be supplied from the Morrison Institute, or from other quarters where they have been brought up with Christian principles, and from these elementary schools on the other hand would be taken those pupils who would be likely to derive advantage from a superior education in the Morrison Institution.

It may here be observed that as the new system will admit of the course of eight years study being reduced to a shorter period, a greater number of pupils will annually be prepared for quitting the School and entering their future career.

It would also be desirable to devise some plan for the useful employment of the boys after their course of education is completed. As yet, however, the Trustees are only able to state that it will be their endeavor to place with the different Missionary bodies in China those who are eligible for and disposed to be employed in that field of usefulness, and to find for others some suitable and useful occupation.

With regard to interference with the Religious prejudices of the Chinese, the School Committee in their Report to Government state "that there is no need for apprehension on this score. No persons seem less bigoted than the Chinese in their attachment to their system of religious belief, and they have proved in most cases willing to allow their children to receive religious instruction and to receive it themselves."

The present expenses of the Society, amount to about $4000 per annum and for this sum, with the exception of about $900, the Trustees have to depend entirely upon annual contributions from the foreign residents in China.

Owing to the absence of Dr. Bridgeman from Canton, the usual collections were only partially made there last year, and in Hong Kong and at the Northern Ports the subscriptions have also been limited in consequence of the objects of the Society being as yet imperfectly understood. From those and other circumstances, the Society will it is feared be unable to meet the expenses of the current year without more general support.

The Trustees feel assured that the motives which have hitherto induced individuals to give their aid to the Society will now lead them to come forward to give renewed impulse to its efforts at a time when its sphere of usefulness is likely to be so much extended, and they doubt not that others will cheerfully recognize the obligation which rests upon each of us to contribute to the temporal and spiritual welfare of their fellow creatures, and of those in particular among whom Providence has placed us.

It may also with reason, be expected that such efforts will tend speedily to remove the many prejudices entertained by the Chinese against Foreigners to extend our intercourse with them, to advance Commerce and civilization, and to open a new field of usefulness to Missionary labor.

A subscription is wanted for two objects, the Morrison Society and the Elementary School. It is calculated that if all in Victoria, Canton, and Shanghai subscribe, sufficient funds for the two objects will be obtained. It is hoped therefore that all will give, however small the contribution may be.

They will have thereby the satisfaction of aiding to promote the grand objects at present contemplated, particularly of giving education to a vast number of children now totally neglected, and of sowing among a large population the seeds of morality and religon, which, with the blessing of Providence, may lead to a plentiful harvest, and extend its benefits far and wide.

Michigan Papers in Chinese Studies

No. 1 The Chinese Economy, 1912-1949, by Albert Feuerwerker

No. 2 The Cultural Revolution: 1967 in Review, four essays by Michel Oksenberg, Carl Riskin, Robert Scalapino, and Ezra Vogel

No. 3 Two Studies in Chinese Literature, by Li Chi and Dale Johnson

No. 4 Early Communist China: Two Studies, by Ronald Suleski and Daniel Bays

No. 5 The Chinese Economy, ca. 1870-1911, by Albert Feuerwerker

No. 6 Chinese Paintings in Chinese Publications, 1956-1868: An Annotated Bibliography and an Index to the Paintings, by E.J. Laing

No. 7 The Treaty Ports and China's Modernization: What Went Wrong?, by Rhoads Murphey

No. 8 Two Twelfth Century Texts on Chinese Painting, by Robert Junji Maeda

No. 9 The Economy of Communist China, 1949-1969, by Chu-yuan Cheng

No. 10 Educated Youth and the Cultural Revolution in China, by Martin Singer

No. 11 Premodern China: A Bibliographical Introduction, by Chun-shu Chang

No. 12 Two Studies on Ming History, by Charles O. Hucker

Michigan Abstracts of Chinese and Japanese Works on Chinese History

No. 1 The Ming Tribute Grain System, by Hoshi Ayao

No. 2 Commerce and Society in Sung China, by Shiba Yoshinobu

Available from the Center for Chinese Studies, The University of Michigan, 104 Lane Hall, Ann Arbor, Michigan 48104.

